Bearing Witness in Acts and Today

Bearing Witness in Acts and Today

TROY M. TROFTGRUBEN

CASCADE *Books* • Eugene, Oregon

BEARING WITNESS IN ACTS AND TODAY

Copyright © 2025 Troy M. Troftgruben. All rights reserved. Except for brief quotations in critical publications or reviews, no part of this book may be reproduced in any manner without prior written permission from the publisher. Write: Permissions, Wipf and Stock Publishers, 199 W. 8th Ave., Suite 3, Eugene, OR 97401.

Cascade Books
An Imprint of Wipf and Stock Publishers
199 W. 8th Ave., Suite 3
Eugene, OR 97401

www.wipfandstock.com

PAPERBACK ISBN: 978-1-6667-5412-4
HARDCOVER ISBN: 978-1-6667-5413-1
EBOOK ISBN: 978-1-6667-5414-8

Cataloguing-in-Publication data:

Names: Troftgruben, Troy M.

Title: Bearing witness in Acts and today / Troy M. Troftgruben.

Description: Eugene, OR: Cascade Books, 2025 | Includes bibliographical references.

Identifiers: ISBN 978-1-6667-5412-4 (paperback) | ISBN 978-1-6667-5413-1 (hardcover) | ISBN 978-1-6667-5414-8 (ebook)

Subjects: LCSH: Bible. Acts—Criticism, interpretation, etc. | Evangelistic work | Missions—Biblical teaching

Classification: BS2625.52 T76 2025 (paperback) | BS2625.52 (ebook)

VERSION NUMBER 05/13/25

Unless noted otherwise, Scripture quotations are from the New Revised Standard Version Updated Edition of the Bible, copyright © 2022 by the division of Christian Education of the National Council of the Churches of Christ in the USA. Used by permission. All rights reserved.

To my students at Wartburg Theological Seminary,
whose questions about Scripture and ministry
first fanned the flames of this book

Contents

Acknowledgments | ix
List of Abbreviations | xi
Introduction | xiii

1 Embracing the Story | 1
2 Telling the Story | 18
3 Embodying the Story | 35
4 Making the Story Public | 53
5 Conversing About the Story | 74
6 Taking the Story to New Places | 93
7 Sharing the Story as a Way of Life | 115

Conclusion: A Word of Promise | 132
Bibliography | 143

Acknowledgments

Writing is never a solo endeavor—certainly not for me. Many have assisted, informed, and inspired me on this journey. Without them, you wouldn't be reading this.

I am grateful for Cascade Books at Wipf & Stock, specifically George Callihan for his assistance, Rodney Clapp for his gracious encouragement to me, and Matthew Wimer for his prompt and fair dealings with my late changes and revisions.

I am indebted to many friends and colleagues who read portions of this book. Miguel Gomez-Acosta raised great questions and areas for tweaking, often by texting me at odd hours of the day. His commitment to faithful witness and friendship to me will not be forgotten. Erika Uthe took time from a sabbatical to read most of this manuscript, giving helpful insights from her work with church leaders and communities. And Philip Hirsch raised very thoughtful questions about the language of bearing witness and the ways people hear that language today.

I give thanks to members of a writers' group that meets at Charlotte's Coffee House in Dubuque—especially Susanna Cantu Gregory, Martin Lohrmann, and Benjamin Winter—with whom I shared several chapters of this book. They not only influenced my thinking and writing, but they have been a source of support and friendship for a decade.

I am indebted to Susan Dub, my sister, for proofreading the full manuscript of this book before its printing. Everyone needs a big sister like her, who has done as much for me as she has over the years.

I give thanks for Wartburg Theological Seminary, especially President Kristin Johnston Largen, Dean Cheryl Peterson, and my faculty colleagues, who have all been supportive of my ongoing research and work.

Acknowledgments

I am deeply grateful for my students at Wartburg Theological Seminary—to whom this book is dedicated—especially those who have participated in my Acts course and there contributed to my thinking. It has been their interest in the theme of bold witness that first inspired this project.

Finally, I am most grateful to my wife, Maria, and to my children, Timothy and Teresa, for grounding, supporting, and encouraging me throughout the ups and downs of writing. I would not be able to do such work without their companionship on the way.

List of Abbreviations

Abbreviations and citation conventions follow *The SBL Handbook of Style: For Biblical Studies and Related Disciplines*, edited by Billie Jean Collins et al., 2nd ed. (Atlanta: SBL, 2014). The following abbreviations are regularly used throughout this book:

ABD *Anchor Bible Dictionary.* Edited by David Noel Freedman. 6 vols. New York: Doubleday, 1992.

ANF *The Ante-Nicene Fathers*, edited by Alexander Roberts and James Donaldson. 10 vols. 1885–1887. Repr., Grand Rapids: Eerdmans, 1951.

BDAG Walter Bauer, Frederick W. Danker, W. F. Arndt, and F. W. Gingrich. *Greek-English Lexicon of the New Testament and Other Early Christian Literature.* 3rd ed. Chicago: University of Chicago Press, 2000.

ELCA The Evangelical Lutheran Church of America

LW *Luther's Works.* American ed. Edited by Jaroslav Pelikan and Helmut Lehmann. 55 vols. St. Louis and Philadelphia: Concordia and Fortress, 1955–86.

LXX The Septuagint, the Greek translation of the Hebrew Bible (Old Testament)

NRSVue The New Revised Standard Version, updated edition

List of Abbreviations

OCD   *Oxford Classical Dictionary.* Edited by Simon Hornblower and Antony Spawforth. 4th ed. Oxford: Oxford University Press, 2012.

TDNT   *Theological Dictionary of the New Testament.* Edited by Gerhard Kittel and Gerhard Friedrich. Translated by Geoffrey W. Bromiley. 10 vols. Grand Rapids: Eerdmans, 1964–76.

Introduction

> But you will receive power when the Holy Spirit has come upon you, and you will be my witnesses in Jerusalem, in all Judea and Samaria, and to the ends of the earth.
>
> —Acts 1:8[1]

WHAT DOES FAITHFUL WITNESS look like?

For over a decade, I have taught seminary courses on Acts. At each semester's end, I regularly ask: what in Acts do we most need to ponder further today?

Across my classes, the most frequent response is "bold witness." It's both a characteristic and an activity of Jesus-followers in Acts. It's also something many of my students do not associate with their experiences of church communities today. This theme in Acts makes them ponder, imagine, and wonder.

For many Christians in the Western world, what faithful witness looks like today is a question without clear answers. Whether or not it's "bold," a clear, working sense of what faithful witness is today would be a fine start. Whatever language we use—be it traditional (evangelism) or progressive (advocacy) or churchy (gospel sharing) or more individualistic (testifying) or more communal (public witness)—just what it means to bear witness faithfully to the gospel today is increasingly complex and unclear.

---

1. Unless otherwise noted, all quoted Scripture passages in this book are from the New Revised Standard Version updated edition (NRSVue).

Introduction

Some people, in fact, might question whether it matters. I once led a congregational education forum on the witness of early church communities at which I posed the question: "How are Christians called to live distinctively today?" Their reactions were largely negative: "Why should they live distinctively?" "What is their motive?" "Why should Christians draw any distinctions at all?" Their questions were fueled largely by negative experiences with judgmental or aggressive forms of evangelism. Underneath these questions resided a deep uncertainty, if not apathy, about the call of Jesus to be witnesses today.

For many people, the most complicating factor is past experiences of evangelism practices that have been manipulative, harmful, and hurtful. In North America and elsewhere, Christians have practiced evangelism in imperialist or colonialist ways to mold others into their image, to reinforce cultural inequalities, and to support hierarchical distinctions. In the distant and not-so-distant past, people have used the Christian faith to support land conquest, slaveholding, gender discrimination, patriarchal norms, religious persecution, and even genocidal practices. And the wounds from these experiences run very, very deep.

The realities and repercussions of these experiences are not simply part of a bygone past. Pastor and social activist William Barber II describes his experiences of some Christians who bear the name evangelical:

> So-called white evangelicals, who say so much about what God says so little—and so little about what God says so much—have dominated public discourse about religion in America for my entire adult life. They have insisted that faith is not political, except when it comes to prayer in school, abortion, homosexuality, and property rights. They have overlooked the more than 2,500 verses in Scripture that have to do with love, justice, and care for the poor, and they have tried to make Jesus an honorary member of the NRA. What these so-called evangelicals have done is nothing short of theological malpractice.[2]

Barber is not alone in his frustration with the practices of some Christians, especially those less sensitive to the harm that some others have experienced from well-intended church people. For this reason, some people today have negative reactions to the language of "evangelical," since—rightly or wrongly—they associate it with practices like judgmental messaging, traditionalist readings of Scripture, apathy to racial justice, and forms of

2. Barber, "Foreword," 5.

Introduction

conservative partisan politics.[3] These associations, from wherever they come, prompt some to be uncomfortable with the language and even idea of being evangelical in any sense of the word today.

And yet, despite the sins, shortcomings, and shortsightedness of Christians past and present, the call of Jesus to be his witnesses remains. In fact, it matters even more.

In a world uncertain and confused about whether the gospel of Jesus is good news, the call to faithful witness matters. In a world scarred by racism, sexism, and discrimination in God's name, the call to share the good news of Jesus matters. In a world abounding in religious paths and unhealthy idols, faithful witness in the name of Jesus matters. Whatever language is used, the world needs to hear good news in the name of Jesus spoken, embodied, and made known in ways that are truly good news for them.

Whether or not followers of Jesus today are called to embrace and reclaim evangelical language, they are called *to be* evangelical in the original and most generous sense of the word, as a people centered in, dedicated to, and changed by the gospel.

Acts and Bearing Witness Today

What does it look like for the people of God to bear faithful witness to the good news of Jesus in the world today?

The story of Acts informs and speaks to this question. In the oldest narrative of the early church, we find a story about a community that holds together complex tensions in fascinating ways. We find communities bearing witness boldly, not brashly, to a life-changing experience of good news. We find a church that shares the gospel, not just in words, but also in deeds. We find a gospel message that inspires change, but not in ways that adhere to conventional patterns.

In this narrative, we find faithful witnesses among both famous apostles and anonymous believers. We find individuals who do not excel at sharing the gospel, but who do it anyway. We find people speaking publicly about Jesus, only after some persuasive pestering by the Holy Spirit. We find individuals making mistakes and a church struggling to be the

---

3. Even among those who identify as "Evangelical" (part of American Evangelicalism), an increasing number wish to distance themselves from this language (Darling, "Evangelical").

witnesses Jesus calls them to be. But their mistakes are no obstacle to God's faithfulness making fruitful their efforts.

Despite its full title (the Acts of the Apostles), this narrative is a story not about heroic human beings, but about *God*. Similarly, its depiction of faithful witness is not a story about human heroism as much as it is about divine empowerment. Although human beings get involved, the initiative and energy for witness all stem from God's Holy Spirit. From start to finish, the evangelical activity of faithful witness is not a human achievement, but a work of God by the Holy Spirit.

Given this, we might approach this topic the way we approach the story of Acts: with focus on God. Tempted as we are to concentrate on what *we can do* to be faithful witnesses—strategies, tactics, programs, practices, experiments—we are called first to consider what *God has done, is doing,* and *may do*. After all, the effects of sharing the message of Jesus hinge less upon us and our efforts than upon the power of the message itself. It is our story's subject matter—the good news of God in Jesus Christ—that makes our witness significant, effective, and fruitful.

A friend of mine was once asked to teach an evangelism course at a seminary. He found it challenging, since he found scarcely any resources to assist him. "No one whom I know and trust is teaching this," he told me. Those who gave him input only offered negations—things he should *not* do.

Many of us may feel similarly surrounded more by negations than constructive ideas about faithful witness today, leaving us at a loss. This is why I write this book: to invite us to reengage the story of Acts in a way that expands our imagination and sparks our creativity about the diverse ways faithful witness take place in this narrative—and may take place today.

Toward (Not So) New Language: Bearing Witness

Conventionally, sharing the message of Jesus has been called "evangelism." This language is rich and provocative.

Underneath it is a Greek word (*euangelion*) meaning "good news." The same word lies behind several other English words: evangel, evangelical, evangelistic, and evangelize. In the US in recent years, these words have become heavily associated with Evangelicalism, a movement of Protestant Christianity marked by emphasis on life-changing conversion, Scripture as sole authority, and more conservative theology.[4] The movement of

---

4. Like the words "catholic" and "orthodox," the word "evangelical" only refers to

Introduction

Evangelical Christianity has also traditionally invested more heavily in conventional practices of evangelism, further associating evangelism with Evangelicalism. As a result, evangelism language provokes reactions among hearers in ways that may have nothing to do with its original meaning. For example, a congregation I served once offered an adult education session on "Evangelism." It was sparsely attended. The same congregation later offered virtually the same session under a different title: "Contagious Christianity." The attendance quadrupled.

As this book's title implies, I like the language "bearing witness" more than evangelism, for several reasons.

1. It comes from Scripture, especially the narrative of Acts.
2. It lacks the baggage of "evangelism," inviting a fresh look at an enduring call.
3. The language is holistic and personal. It refers not to parroting stock information, but to speaking from one's personal experience, which involves our whole selves.
4. The language implies truth-telling. To bear witness is to give a clearer and fuller glimpse of the truth. This is a helpful metaphor for the pluralistic and inequitable world in which we live, since it implies not just a religious message but also truthful, transparent, and conscientious messaging about sacred realities.

For these reasons, I think the language of bearing witness helps us think differently about the call to share the message of Jesus. And if there is a topic of Christian faith today that invites a fresh approach, it is evangelism.

Bearing witness is language that carries many different shades of meaning today. Depending on the context, it can mean issuing a formal witness statement, sharing personal experiences, advocating publicly for underrepresented voices, attesting to injustice suffered, confirming something's truthfulness, or affirming another's experience by listening.[5] The diverse ways of understanding this language pose a risk of muddying its meaning.

---

a distinctive church body/group when capitalized. In American English, the capitalized word "Evangelical" typically refers to the distinctive movement of Evangelicalism, whereas the uncapitalized "evangelical" may refer to any practice or movement that emphasizes or prioritizes the gospel and its sharing in theology and practice.

5. In public discourse around injustice, bearing witness typically refers to giving voice to suffered injustice (see, for example, Richardson, *Bearing Witness While Black*; Kerns and Moore, *Bearing Witness*). In psychology, bearing witness typically refers to the

However, at its core, bearing witness simply means testifying to one's experience. The language is tied originally and especially to court settings, where witnesses attest to what they have seen in relation to scrutinized activity. Their testimonies help corroborate the truth and correct false information. Outside judicial settings, people may bear witness in similar ways to unjust events, distinctive experiences, or personal trauma. In all these scenarios, bearing witness seeks to make the truth more fully known and to call into question untruths in circulation.

In Christian contexts, bearing witness is associated with sharing a message about Jesus, but it also taps into personal experience. Like testimony in a courtroom setting, it invites people to share not abstractly, but from what they have known and experienced. To bear witness means to offer eyewitness testimony that this good news is good not just in theory, but also on a personal level.

Bearing witness also strives for a more just and accurate depiction of the truth. Like testimony in public settings, witness about the faith of Jesus tries to make what is true about it more fully known. In society at large, there is growing awareness of the importance of public protest and testimony about injustice, especially by those negatively affected. As their examples show, acts of truth-telling have the power to change mindsets and outcomes. In the same way, amid the misconceptions, stereotypes, and falsehoods about the Christian faith now circulating in society, true testimony by people of faith helps to portray its content and character more accurately and honestly. In other words, bearing witness to the gospel entails not only testifying to its goodness, but also offering a clearer and fuller portrayal of what this faith truly is.

Why This Matters

I write this book because Jesus invites his followers to be his witnesses in the world—and many of us struggle to know what this means.

---

sharing of personal experiences, especially traumatic ones (see, for example, Pikiewicz, "Power and Strength of Bearing Witness"). In counseling, bearing witness often refers to the practice of affirming another's experiences by listening (see, for example, J. Johnson, "Power of Bearing Witness"). In Zen tradition, bearing witness also refers to listening, but with added emphasis on the transformative aspects of self-emptying and compassion (see, for example, Glassman, *Bearing Witness: A Zen Master's Lessons*).

INTRODUCTION

First, many of us have forgotten that faithful witness is part of our DNA and heritage as Jesus' people.[6] No matter what denominational brand of Christianity with which we identify, faithful witness is part of our history and heritage. Throughout the earliest traditions of the Gospels, Jesus calls, trains, and sends out his followers to engage the surrounding world intentionally with his message.[7]

The narrative of Acts spotlights this in its opening scene. Gathered with his followers, Jesus issues them a special call: "you will receive power when the Holy Spirit has come upon you, and you will be my witnesses in Jerusalem, in all Judea and Samaria, and to the ends of the earth" (1:8). The call to be his witnesses is reiterated throughout Acts, as Jesus' followers enter new spaces in his name. In fact, the story concludes on the note of witness "in an unhindered manner" (28:31), suggesting it remains in full force as the narrative ends—with readers and hearers invited to join in the movement themselves. Although a story of history, Acts is less about a bygone heroic era than it is a story of origins—a story about where we (as the church) came from and who we are. In view of this, attending to Jesus' call to be his witnesses is not a matter of history, but one of reclaiming our legacy. It is a matter of embracing who we are.

Second, many of us have been soured by bad examples. We can name negative experiences of evangelism more readily than positive ones. And unfortunately, the negative experiences stick with us longer. Not long ago, as part of our summer vacation, I took my family to Disneyland. Camped just outside the park gates were a couple street preachers, sporting "Repent or Perish" T-shirts. They preached by amplified speaker several hours a day. Although their spoken words were gentler than their T-shirts, their strategy was poor. As I ushered my kids to the highlight of their summer, loud preachers pressed us and other family groups to turn or burn.

Was this strategy truly a glimpse of the gospel's goodness? Their position created a fork in the path, between the Disneyland entrance and their street pulpit, forcing the passerby to prioritize one or the other. Aside from

---

6. A 2018 Barna study reports that most churchgoers have not heard of the Great Commission (Matt 28:18–20)—and much less know its significance (Barna, "51% of Churchgoers"). While familiarity with one passage is a relatively superficial marker, it still reflects unawareness of key places in Scripture where Jesus invites followers to engage the world intentionally.

7. Mark 3:13–19a (so also Matt 10:1–4; Luke 6:12–16); Mark 6:6b–13 (so also Matt 10:1–14; Luke 9:1–6); Matt 9:37–38; 28:18–20; Luke 10:1–12; 24:45–49; John 20:21–22; Acts 1:6–8. See also Mark 16:15–20.

an occasional "Amen," no one acknowledged the preachers. If their goal was conversation, the approach failed. If their goal was to urge people to refrain (or repent) from going to Disneyland, it was terribly timed. If their goal was merely broadcasting, they probably felt smug and satisfied. I hear that on other days preachers with harsher messaging occupy the corner.[8] And I realize anew why some people have negative impressions of Christianity.

Street Preachers, Author's Photo

I still ponder this experience—and ask how people of faith can offer a more constructive witness. While many of us struggle with how to engage our world faithfully, starting with condemnation only burns bridges. In a

---

8. Although I saw no clear signs of it in these individuals, many street preachers set up outside Disneyland to protest or preach against Disney's support of the LGBTQIA+ community.

Introduction

world increasingly aware of how Christianity has historically contributed to forms of dehumanizing, the call of Jesus invites us to do better. The world needs faithful witness to the gospel that is more thoughtful, sensitive, relational, and vulnerable.

Third, many of us are afraid our attempts will go badly—or cause harm. While we may care about faithful witness, taking concrete steps is another matter. Since many of us lack awareness of good examples, we don't know what it looks like. Many of us lack experience talking about or doing things in the name of our faith, making us afraid to start. Many of us are aware of insensitive and harmful evangelism strategies, making us afraid to be associated with them. Most of all, an increasing number of us are afraid of introducing awkwardness to existing relationships or coming across as judgmental. According to recent research, the biggest reason Christians in the US today are reluctant to talk about their faith is that they do not wish to provoke tensions or arguments.[9]

At the end of the day, most of us are reluctant to concern ourselves with constructive witness to our faith because we fear it will go badly. But faithful witness is not an extracurricular activity as much as an outgrowth from who we are as people of faith. More than anything, faithful witness needs to be authentic to ourselves, to our personalities, and to our experiences. In other words, it should spring organically from who we are. It entails being open and honest about something that gives us joy without requiring specific responses from others. It involves a willingness to reflect with others on something significant, in ways that are genuine to who we are.

Fourth and final, many of us don't realize that faithful witness can take a wide diversity of forms. Influenced by negative experiences of certain strategies, many of us let our imagination and creativity shut down. In doing so, we give faithful witness over to the brash and outspoken voices already out there. But engaging the world in Jesus' name is not restricted to a one-size-fits-all approach. In fact, at the earliest stages of the church, as seen in the narrative of Acts, we see a variety of approaches to faithful witness at work, as the ensuing chapters of this book make clear. The witness of

---

9. At 28 percent of respondents (Barna, "Why People"). The second most common reason among Christians is "I don't feel like I know enough" (17 percent). The response "I'm not religious and don't care about these kinds of topics" (23 percent) is more reflective of non-Christians. Recent research suggests this general reluctance to talk about faith may be waning, at least among Generation Z (see Barna, "Actions, Invitations, Storytelling").

early church communities and people in Acts is diverse, dynamic, and far more complex than a superficial reading may appreciate.

A diversity of approaches is especially needed for the changing world in which we live. Over the last few decades, many changes have happened for church communities: decreases in membership/affiliation, shifts in worship attendance, and changing practices of generosity, just to name a few. At the same time, growth in religious pluralism, relativism, secularism, and atheism in Western societies has made for major shifts like decreased interest across society in religious faith.[10] Amid these shifts, Christian convictions about the significance of faithful witness have generally decreased.[11] At the same time, research suggests that, among religious and nonreligious people, the most welcome and hospitable opportunity to explore the Christian faith is in the context of casual, one-on-one conversation.[12] While convictions have shifted among Christians regarding the significance of sharing their faith, the need for faithful, sensitive, and constructive witness to the faith of Jesus continues today.

What This Book Is About

This book reengages the call of Jesus in Acts to bear witness faithfully. The book explores how witness takes shape in Acts, why that matters, and what that might mean for today. Each chapter focuses on Scripture passages from Acts, examples of the early church engaged in witness, and reflections on faithful witness today. Nearly all Scripture passages appear in the Revised Common Lectionary for worship, making them more familiar. Each chapter concludes with discussion questions, resources, and suggestions. These resources allow readers to engage in Scripture and reflection, as individuals and as communities, about faithful witness today.

Chapter 1 ("Embracing the Story") explores the starting point of faithful witness: the call of Jesus in Scripture and its impact upon our lives. The closing chapter of Luke's Gospel and the opening chapter of Acts are key sources for this call, showing how it starts with people's lived experiences of Jesus and the message about him. That is, faithful witness entails speaking

---

10. Barna, "Atheism Doubles."

11. According to Barna ("Sharing Faith"), in 1993 nearly 90 percent of US Christians believed "every Christian has a responsibility to share their faith," but in 2018—twenty-five years later—that percentage dropped to less than two-thirds (64 percent).

12. Barna, "Beyond an Invitation."

INTRODUCTION

from our experiences in ways that show the gospel's personal significance. A practical step this chapter suggests is taking stock of our own spiritual journeys, to help us speak authentically (vs. artificially) about the gospel from our lived experiences of faith.

Chapter 2 ("Telling the Story") considers what it means to bear witness to the story of Jesus through words. A focus text for this is the story of Pentecost (Acts 2), which associates the arrival of the Holy Spirit with speaking in ways others can understand. The chapter discusses how the miracle of Pentecost is one that promotes diversity, not uniformity. It also considers the variety of ways in which talking about faith can take shape, not only for the sake of others but also for the sake of our own faith. A practical step proposed by this chapter is the practice of testimony in the context of worship.

Chapter 3 ("Embodying the Story") considers what it means to share the story of Jesus through our actions. Focal texts are Acts 2:42–47 and 4:32–37, which portray the earliest communities of believers as engaged in activity that quickly earned the favor and goodwill of their neighbors. The chapter explores ways that early churches created positive impressions upon outsiders by their benevolent deeds, care for the impoverished, and positive contributions to society. These activities were neither arbitrary nor random—they embodied and lived out the practices first seen in Jesus' life and ministry. A practical step noted in this chapter is to consider the diverse ways in which our individual and communal witness might have more intentional engagement with our world.

Chapter 4 ("Making the Story Public") explores what faithful witness might look like in public spaces, in view of examples of public witness among early church communities. A focal story is from Acts 3–4, where Peter and John cannot "keep from speaking" publicly about Jesus (Acts 4:20), empowered by a boldness inspired by the Holy Spirit. The chapter also highlights how early church communities, in their early years, inhabited and made wide use of public spaces (e.g., temples, marketplaces, outdoor spaces). As a community less anchored to specific buildings, it was known as "the Way," suggesting a way of life more than a particular group or location. Some practical suggestions for public witness are given, which diversely reflect concerns for justice, for marginalized peoples, and for bridge-building.

Chapter 5 ("Conversing About the Story") identifies how faithful witness often takes shape through conversations and dialogue with others. This approach to witness prioritizes others' questions, concerns, and agency in the conversation—more than preconceived answers. A focal text is Acts 8:26–40 (Philip and the Ethiopian), which offers an example of evangelism that is conversational, collaborative, oriented around questions, and grounded in Scripture. The story depicts witness taking shape in ways that give agency and ownership to others. A practical suggestion is to bring topics of ultimate significance related to faith into everyday conversations, inviting others into meaningful and authentic dialogue.

Chapter 6 ("Taking the Story to New Places") eyes how the call to faithful witness compels us to enter new spaces and places for the sake of engaging others. A focal text is Acts 10:1—11:18, featuring Peter's call to share the good news with Cornelius and his household. The story showcases human reluctance to enter new places, the forcefulness of the Holy Spirit's leading, and the ways the Spirit leads God's people into deeper discernment about their calling. The chapter highlights how the story of Acts is not about human initiative as much as a people trying not to get in the way of the Spirit's courageous leading. A practical step for today is practices of spiritual discernment, which can help clarify where the Spirit is leading individuals and communities today. Like Peter, we may be led by the Spirit to embrace intentionally people otherwise othered and disenfranchised by faith communities.

Chapter 7 ("Sharing the Story as a Way of Life") considers how faithful witness calls us to translate the good news of Jesus into language that makes sense to people, without guaranteed results. A focal text is Acts 17:16–34 (Paul in Athens), which features Paul speaking about Jesus in less conventional language, without losing the substance of the gospel. Like Paul's audience in Athens, many religiously "unaffiliated" people today have interests in spirituality, ethics, and contributing to a greater good. They just need exposure to constructive witness that affirms their journeys, their identities, their questions, and their experiences. A practical suggestion for today is to consider the interests and concerns of unaffiliated people in our world more conscientiously, with an openness to the ways it may prompt us to engage in more intentional witness.

The conclusion ("A Word of Promise") rounds out the book by reflecting on changes and uncertainties related to faithful witness in society and the world today. A focal text is the ending of Acts (28:16–31), especially its closing scene (vv. 30–31), which is understood here as a word of promise, not simply a call to action. Even though changes and challenges abound for faithful witness today, we find in Acts a God who empowers and enables us to

INTRODUCTION

bear faithful witness, aided by the Spirit's presence. We are invited to join this movement of bold witness, whose ultimate conclusion is yet to be written.

Reclaiming a Legacy

The denomination of which I am part is the Evangelical Lutheran Church of America (ELCA). It has a conflicted relationship with the first adjective of its name: evangelical.

The word reflects the church's German Protestant roots. Martin Luther and his colleagues called their churches "evangelische" (evangelical) to highlight the gospel's central place in their teaching. Only their opponents called them "Lutheran," and Martin Luther adamantly opposed it.[13] To this day, the Protestant church in Germany identifies itself as the Evangelische (evangelical) church—not the Lutherische (Lutheran) church. Dozens of Lutheran bodies across the globe continue to use the same language (evangelical) to honor the same historic connection.[14]

The word "evangelical" marks more than just a historic connection. It signifies ongoing commitment to the gospel as central to the life of faith. That's what makes it so great a word—and one so widely used (not just by Lutherans). In the last half-century, as the word became heavily associated with US Evangelicalism, confusion has resulted. When people see "evangelical" in my denomination's name, they often assume it signifies a social or ethical conservatism, an emphasis on conversion, and limited regard for ecumenical church tradition. Although both Evangelicalism and the ELCA are deeply committed to the gospel, they are so in very different ways. As a result, many in my denomination feel conflicted about "evangelical" language, though in my experience most are more interested in reclaiming it than dropping it.

Like my denomination, the church at large today has a comparably conflicted relationship with evangelism, as it is conventionally understood. We believe Jesus calls us, as the church, to bear witness to the good news. But we are afraid of being like the negative examples we have seen. We are afraid of causing harm by being insensitive to people's beliefs and experiences. We are afraid that others will misunderstand us as overbearing or judgmental. When it comes to bearing witness, we struggle with where to start.

---

13. "Admonition Against Insurrection," *LW* 45:70–71. See also "On Receiving Both Kinds," *LW* 36:266; "Christian Letter of Consolation," *LW* 43:112.
14. Blezard, "'E' Word."

Introduction

In Scripture we find a Jesus who calls imperfect followers to invest in faithful witness, however clumsy and imperfect their methods. We find a Jesus who promises to accompany those who strive for faithful witness. Whatever our knee-jerk reactions are to evangelism and evangelical traditions, we are called as church to embrace and reclaim our legacy of bearing witness in the world. Somehow, part of us may resonate with the experience of early believers who attested: "we cannot keep from speaking about what we have seen and heard" (Acts 4:20). We are just not sure where to start.

If these words inspire something within you, read on. Let's hear the call of Jesus anew in the pages of Acts.

Questions for Discussion

1. What images come to your mind as you hear the word "evangelism"?
2. What initial reactions do you have to the language "bearing witness"? Do you find this introduction's reasoning for the language persuasive?
3. On a scale of one to ten (1 = unimportant; 10 = extremely important), how important do you think it is for Christians to engage in faithful witness today?
4. In your experience, what are the greatest obstacles for Christians engaging in faithful witness today?
5. Think of a good example of Christian witness you have experienced. What made it constructive?

Resources for Further Exploration

- Barna. "Atheism Doubles Among Generation Z." January 24, 2018. https://www.barna.com/research/atheism-doubles-among-generation-z/.
- ———. "Beyond an Invitation to Church: Opportunities for Faith-Sharing." March 26, 2019. https://www.barna.com/research/opportunities-for-faith-sharing/.
- Bateza, Anthony. "Beyond Evangelism: Sharing What Matters." *Living Lutheran*, March 26, 2024. https://www.livinglutheran.org/2024/03/beyond-evangelism-sharing-what-matters/.

- Jacobson, Harold. *Rockin' the Front Porch: Sharing the Faith in the New Normal.* Morrisville, NC: Lulu, 2020.
- Skinner, Matthew L. *Acts: Catching Up With the Spirit.* Nashville: Abingdon, 2020.
- Thomason, Steve. *A Cartoonist's Guide to Acts: A Full-Color Graphic Novel.* A Cartoonist's Guide to the Bible. Self-published, 2023.

Action Steps for Further Consideration

- Invite a friend or two to join you in reading and discussing this book. Make plans for an enjoyable setting for group discussion on a regular basis.
- Google the following words and phrases: evangelism, evangelical, bearing witness, Christian witness. What impressions and images are associated with this language?
- Check out whether your church community has staff, committee, or projects dedicated to the work of evangelism. If you know someone who serves (or has served) in leadership of one of these initiatives, interview that person about the challenges and joys of this work today.
- Consider whether you know someone who bears witness to the Christian faith in admirable ways. Ask the person about this. Why do they go about it as they do?

1

Embracing the Story

> One of the tragedies of our life is that we keep forgetting who we are and waste a lot of time and energy to prove what doesn't need to be proved. We are God's beloved daughters and sons, not because we have proven ourselves worthy of God's love, but because God freely chose us.
>
> —Henri J. M. Nouwen[1]

My seminary internship took place at a congregation with connections to an addiction recovery center. As part of that, I worked with church leaders to lead a weekly chapel service at the center. Our main contribution was a brief sermon. After several months, I learned something significant.

Most weeks, the sermons spoke generally about things. Since most preachers had limited connection to those gathered, doing more was tough. Most weeks, the sermons were not home runs. One week I decided to change it up. Using Acts 1:1–8, I talked about the call of Jesus to bear witness to our lived experience of the faith. To illustrate the point, I shared some of my own story. People looked up and noticed. The sermon went long, but no one seemed to care.

My faith journey is neither dramatic nor impressive. And I meandered quite a bit. But it was authentic. Those present seemed to listen more intently than they had to any chapel sermon for months. Many of the people

---

1. Nouwen, *Here and Now*, 136.

were familiar with Scripture. What they wanted more of was how that story reshaped the course of a specific life—and how that story resonates with their stories. More people wanted to talk with me that day after chapel than ever before.

I don't recommend this as a regular preaching strategy. But that day, in this community, it did something: it made the gospel tangible to people who had heard it many times before. It invited imagination about how the gospel makes a difference in daily life. It was one way (among others) of reflecting how the message of Jesus is good news for daily life today.

"You Will Be My Witnesses" (Acts 1:1–11)

This book reengages the call of Jesus to bear witness in the world. That call appears primarily in the story of Luke-Acts, especially Acts.[2]

Many people think Acts is a story about prominent preachers and large crowds, due in part to the familiarity of Pentecost (Acts 2). That assumption not only misses the story's most interesting features; it also ignores how Jesus kicks it off.

Acts 1:1–11 is the narrative's opening overture.[3] It reiterates closing scenes from Luke's Gospel and identifies major themes yet to come.

> 1 In the first book, Theophilus, I wrote about all that Jesus began to do and teach 2 until the day when he was taken up to heaven, after giving instructions through the Holy Spirit to the apostles whom he had chosen. 3 After his suffering he presented himself alive to them by many convincing proofs, appearing to them during forty days and speaking about the kingdom of God. 4 While staying with them, he ordered them not to leave Jerusalem but to wait there for the promise of the Father. "This," he said, "is what you have heard from me; 5 for John baptized with water, but you will be baptized with the Holy Spirit not many days from now." (Acts 1:1–5)

The scene gives a glimpse of Jesus' activity during the forty days between his resurrection and ascension. During this time, he gathers with followers,

---

2. Luke and Acts are widely attributed to the same author due to their abundant commonalities in approach, style, theology, themes, and use of literary genres. For these reasons, I use "Luke" throughout this book as a shorthand reference to the author of Luke and Acts, and "Luke-Acts" as a reference to the collective work of both narratives. For studies more skeptical of the unity of Luke and Acts, see Parsons and Pervo, *Rethinking the Unity*; Walter, *Assumed Authorial Unity*.

3. Noted by Beverly Roberts Gaventa (*Acts*, 66).

presumably on a regular basis, to eat and teach about the reign of God. He also orders them not to leave Jerusalem, but to wait there for the promise of the Father: the Holy Spirit, with whom they will be "baptized" (vv. 4–5).[4] This language does not imply particular sacramental rituals as much as a dynamic empowerment by the Spirit.

On one occasion, Jesus' followers pose a question:

> 6 So when they had come together, they asked him, "Lord, is this the time when you will restore the kingdom to Israel?" 7 He replied, "It is not for you to know the times or periods that the Father has set by his own authority. 8 But you will receive power when the Holy Spirit has come upon you, and you will be my witnesses in Jerusalem, in all Judea and Samaria, and to the ends of the earth." (Acts 1:6–8)

The apostles' question seems to envision the restoration of a golden era from Israel's past. Interestingly, Jesus neither answers nor validates the question. Instead, he deflects its focus: "It is not for you to know the times or periods . . ." (v. 7).

Jesus then identifies what he deems more important about events to come: "you will receive power when the Holy Spirit has come upon you; and you will be my witnesses in Jerusalem, in all Judea and Samaria, and to the ends of the earth" (v. 8).

If Acts has a thesis statement, this is it. First, it gives a basic geographical outline of the ensuing story, from Jerusalem outward. Second, it highlights the major role that the Holy Spirit will have empowering people for ministry. Third, it gives this ministry very distinctive language: Jesus' "witnesses."

What happens after this point brings closure to the scene.

> When he had said this, as they were watching, he was lifted up, and a cloud took him out of their sight. 10 While he was going and they were gazing up toward heaven, suddenly two men in white robes stood by them. 11 They said, "Men of Galilee, why do you stand looking up toward heaven? This Jesus, who has been taken up from you into heaven, will come in the same way as you saw him go into heaven." (Acts 1:9–11)

---

4. Like the dative word *hydati* ("with water") earlier in the sentence, the dative phrase *en pneumati . . . hagiō* is also instrumental ("with the Holy Spirit"). Luke uses the same language in Luke 3:16 and Acts 11:16. So also C. K. Barrett, *Acts*, 1:74; Fitzmyer, *Acts*, 204.

Right after the pronouncement of 1:8, Jesus ascends and is hidden from sight. Two men in white robes appear to tell his followers not to stand around staring, since he will return in similar fashion. Their instructions suggest Jesus' followers are called not to sit around until he returns, but to focus on the purpose he has given—to be his witnesses.

"You Are Witnesses" (Luke 24:48)

Acts 1:1–11 has commonalities with the closing scene of Luke's Gospel, which also features the risen Jesus appearing to followers (Luke 24:33–53).[5] In both Luke 24:33–53 and Acts 1:1–11, Jesus eats with and instructs his followers before ascending. There are differences: in Luke, for example, the gathering happens on Resurrection Sunday, whereas Acts 1 happens after forty days of post-resurrection appearances; further, in Luke Jesus highlights how recent events fulfill Scripture, whereas in Acts he addresses questions about Israel's kingdom.[6] For our purposes, the shared points of emphasis are most important, especially in how Jesus concludes his teaching in each text.

Before ascending, Jesus tells his followers:

> that repentance and forgiveness of sins is to be proclaimed in [the Messiah's] name to all nations, beginning from Jerusalem. You are witnesses of these things. And see, I am sending upon you what my Father promised; so stay here in the city until you have been clothed with power from on high. (Luke 24:47–49)

Like the opening scene of Acts, Jesus concludes his teaching with the same areas of emphasis:

1. Witness (proclamation about Jesus) will go to all nations (Luke 24:47; cf. Acts 1:8)
2. The empowerment of the Holy Spirit (Luke 24:49; cf. Acts 1:5, 8)
3. The call to be Jesus' witnesses (Luke 24:48; cf. Acts 1:8)

At both the end of Luke and the start of Acts, the call to be Jesus' witnesses is central. His followers will be empowered by the Spirit, sent to all nations,

---

5. On Luke 24:33–53 as the ending to Luke's Gospel, see Troftgruben, "Ending of Luke Revisited."

6. Some of these differences may be due to the different rhetorical goals of each story. For fuller discussion of these distinctions, see Parsons, *Departure of Jesus*.

and charged with the calling: "you are/will be witnesses" of Jesus and his saving work (Luke 24:48; Acts 1:8).⁷ With that firmly in place, the stage is set for the story of Acts to begin.

What Witnesses Do

The word "witness"—and its related activity of bearing witness—is comprehensive language for the calling of Jesus in Acts.⁸ At both the end of Luke and the start of Acts, it is the language Jesus uses to orient his followers to this ministry.

On the most basic level, witnesses testify to eyewitness events. Witnesses have specific experiences which they can recount to others. In Greek literature, the word for witness (Greek: *martyr*) first circulated widely in contexts of legal trials and transactions, where people were asked to share eyewitness experiences of things seen and heard.⁹ In classical Athens, witnesses were more valuable sources than written documents.¹⁰ In Jewish tradition, those able to testify who withheld their testimony might be liable before God.¹¹ In the Hebrew Bible (esp. Isaiah 40–55), appeals to witnesses are treated as appeals to objective legal evidence.¹² As in law courts today, in antiquity the testimony of witnesses was evidence strong enough to confirm the truth.

This is the primary meaning of witness in Luke-Acts. It refers to those who saw and experienced Jesus' ministry firsthand. In his Gospel preface, Luke credits his material to those who "from the beginning were

---

7. Acts 1:8: *Esesthe mou martyres* ("you will be my witnesses"). Luke 24:48: *hymeis martyres toutōn* ("You are witnesses of these things").

8. "Witness(es)" (*martyres*): Luke 24:48; Acts 1:8, 22; 2:32; 3:15; 5:32; 10:39, 41; 13:31; 22:15, 20; 26:16. "Bearing witness" (*martyreō, martyromai, apodidomai martyrion/a*): Luke 21:13; Acts 4:33; 14:3; 20:26; 22:18; 23:11; 26:22. The prophets of old also "bore witness" to the events told in Luke's narrative (Acts 10:43; 13:22).

9. See Aeschines, *Timarchus*, 89; Lysias, *Orations* 3.14, §97; 3.20–21, §98; 3.27 §98; Anixemenes of Lampsacus, *Rhetoric to Alexander* 15, 1431b.21; Strathmann, "μάρτυς, μαρτυρέω, μαρτυρία, μαρτύριον," 476.

10. In time, this comparison reversed, but outright mistrust of witnesses was never widespread until after Luke's day, during the later Roman Empire. Keener, *Acts*, 1:694; Todd, "Evidence, Greek and Roman," in *OCD*, 132; Nicholas, "Evidence, Roman," in *OCD*, 132.

11. See, for example, *Shevu'ot* 3:2; *Bava Qamma* 55b–56a.

12. Trites, *Concept of Witness*, 35–65.

eyewitnesses" (1:2).¹³ This grounds his Gospel squarely in authoritative tradition. A similar preference for eyewitnesses appears early in Acts, as followers of Jesus discern how to fill Judas's place. They decide on someone who "accompanied us during all the time that the Lord Jesus went in and out among us, beginning from the baptism of John until the day when he was taken up from us" (1:21–22). And so, early on in Luke-Acts, the role of "witness" is associated with those who accompanied Jesus, making them credible sources of tradition. This resonates with a belief widely held among ancient Mediterranean historians: eyewitness testimony is highly credible.¹⁴ For Luke, those who witnessed Jesus' ministry, death, and resurrection were best equipped to attest to the truthfulness of these events.¹⁵

This primary meaning is worth pondering. At a critical juncture in the story, as Jesus orients his followers to their ministry, he does not call them "preachers," "proclaimers," "spokespeople," or "heralds." Nor does he call them "ambassadors," "prophets," or "priests." Jesus simply calls them "my witnesses"—eyewitnesses to what Jesus has done. As witnesses, they are called to recount their experiences to others. Like witnesses in a court of law, they are not expected to give grand speeches, repeat stock information, or impress audiences with rhetorical skill. Their role is simply to tell what they have seen and heard truthfully.

This is the case in Luke 24, when Jesus first calls his followers witnesses. After recounting how his life, death, and resurrection have fulfilled Scripture, he follows with "you are witnesses of these things" (v. 48). The phrase "these things" refers primarily to Jesus' death and resurrection (v. 46), but also the entirety of his ministry and teaching. So, his followers are not generic witnesses in the abstract. They are witnesses to specific events. They bear witness to specific events related to Jesus that have taken place and fulfilled Scripture.

This notion of witness continues in Acts. As Jesus' followers embrace their role as witnesses, they often speak of their testimony in relation to specific events of Jesus' ministry: they are witnesses to his crucifixion (3:15; 5:32; 10:39b), to his resurrection (1:22; 2:32; 3:15; 5:32; 10:41; 13:31), and finally "to all that he did in Judea and in Jerusalem" (10:39). Their role as

---

13. Here Luke uses the word *autoptēs* ("eyewitness"), which emphasizes firsthand experience even more than *martyres* ("witnesses").

14. See, for example, Herodotus 2.99; Polybius 12.27.1–6; 20.12.8; Aune, *New Testament*, 81.

15. See Acts 1:21–22; 2:32; 3:15; 4:33; 5:32; 10:39, 41; 13:31. Turner, "Every Believer," 61–63 and 66.

witnesses is more than an honorary title. It has a functional purpose in relation to specific events. Having seen Jesus' life, death, and resurrection, they are called to recall and recount these events to others.

Witnesses are experts only in matters related to their firsthand experience. They are not expected to have objective or extensive knowledge about everything. They are expected simply to speak with authority about what they have seen and heard. Jesus' use of this metaphor suggests the same thing for all his followers, of all times and places—not just the original eyewitnesses. They need not be professionally trained speakers, have extensive knowledge, or have the answers to all questions. They are simply called to recall and recount what they have seen, heard, and experienced in relation to Jesus.

The Holistic Nature of Bearing Witness

As the story of Luke-Acts continues, however, it becomes clear there is more to bearing witness than simply repeating a firsthand account of events. It also involves interpreting their significance.

At first, the language of witness refers simply to eyewitnesses of Jesus' ministry (Acts 1:21–22). But soon enough, the community of witnesses expands. Acts refers to Paul, Stephen, and biblical prophets as witnesses who testify to Jesus.[16] As these examples show, the community of Jesus' witnesses grows and expands, and with it the definition of what it means to bear witness to Jesus' saving activity.[17]

In Acts, witnesses testify not just to historical events, but also to *their distinctive experiences* of events related to Jesus and their significance. Paul is a good example. Different from the twelve disciples, Paul was not an eyewitness to Jesus' earthly ministry. Paul, then, is called to bear witness, not as an eyewitness of Jesus' earthly ministry, but in view of what Paul himself has experienced of the risen Jesus. As he recounts his story later, he identifies his calling as testifying to his own experiences of the risen Jesus, years after Jesus' earthly ministry is over:

> Then [Ananias] said [to Paul]: "The God of our ancestors has chosen you to know God's will, *to see* the Righteous One and *to hear* his own voice; for you will be his witness to all the world of *what you have seen and heard*." (Acts 22:14–15, emphasis mine)

16. Acts 10:43; 22:15, 18, 20; 23:11; 26:16, 22.
17. Keener, *Acts*, 1:695–96. Pace Turner, "Every Believer," 57–71.

> But get up and stand on your feet; for I [Jesus] have appeared to you for this purpose, to appoint you to serve and testify *to the things in which you have seen me* and *to those in which I will appear to you*. (Acts 26:16, emphasis mine)

Paul is called to testify to his own encounters with the risen Jesus. This testimony authenticates that Jesus is alive and active. In this way, Paul is not an eyewitness in precisely the same way as the twelve disciples. He is a witness to his own distinctive experiences of the risen Jesus. Paul's testimony is authoritative in a different way that Jesus is alive and at work saving the world.[18]

As these examples from Acts show, bearing witness is a personal and holistic activity. It not only assumes personal experience of events but invites comprehensive engagement with them—on audible, visual, physical, emotional, intellectual, and subjective levels. There is no dimension of human experience that is irrelevant or unimportant.

By way of example, often the most compelling testimonies in a law court are so due to how they interweave many dimensions of experience into a compelling and persuasive account. Different than conventional ideas today of Christian witness as sharing a scripted, generic message, Luke and Acts have a far more holistic vision. They portray faithful witness as speaking from one's own distinctive experiences of who Jesus is, what he has done, and what he has done for us and for all people.

Witnesses Empowered by the Spirit

Luke and Acts use other names for followers of Jesus. Sometimes they are called disciples (*mathētēs*), marking them as learners of Jesus. In Acts they are often called apostles (*apostoloi*), indicating they have been sent out by Jesus.[19] Like the word "witness" (*martyr*), these labels identify people in relation to Jesus and his activity. And yet, more than the other two designations, "witness" clarifies what followers of Jesus are called to do after the

---

18. H. Strathmann observes: "Paul is not a factual witness in the same sense as the older apostles. For he cannot guarantee the story of Christ from first-hand knowledge. He is, however, a witness to truth who seeks to propagate the Christian faith by confession" ("μάρτυς, μαρτυρέω, μαρτυρία, μαρτύριον," 493–94).

19. Luke 6:13; 9:10; 11:49; 17:5; 22:14; 24:10; Acts 1:2, 26; 2:37, 42–43; 4:33, 35–37; 5:2, 12, 18, 29, 40; 6:6; 8:1, 14, 18; 9:27; 11:1; 14:4, 14; 15:2, 4, 6, 22–23; 16:4. The word "apostle" comes from the verb *apostellō*, meaning "send."

first steps of learning and being sent. While continuing to be learners sent into the world, Jesus' followers are called to testify to what they have known and experienced in relation to him.

Espíritu Santo, Fernando de Gorocica, St. Peter's Basilica, Vatican City (March 28, 2021), used with permission, courtesy of Wikimedia Commons

In both Luke 24:33–53 and Acts 1:1–11, Jesus places no prerequisites on his followers' service. He does not say, "if you first prove yourselves in this way" or "if you first do _____." He simply reminds them of his teaching and ministry, then states: "you are/will be (my) witnesses (of these things)." In fact, Jesus focuses not on prerequisites but on empowerment. In both scenes, Jesus weds the call to be witnesses to a promise that the Spirit will enable and equip them to do so faithfully:

> I am sending upon you what my Father promised . . . , power from on high. (Luke 24:49)

> And you will receive power when the Holy Spirit has come upon you. (Acts 1:8a)

Distinctive to Luke-Acts, the Holy Spirit is not a "comforter" but a "power." This power enables Jesus' followers to do what they otherwise cannot do.

The Spirit is a dynamic force who gives the authority, ability, and boldness needed for human beings to answer the call of Jesus faithfully. As Joseph Fitzmyer words it, the Spirit is "the dynamo that activates their testimony."[20] After all, the goal of the Spirit's empowerment is faithful witness. As Justo González points out: "the purpose of the outpouring of the Spirit is not to know the hidden secrets of God, but rather to give witness to Jesus."[21]

Flawed and Fragile Witnesses

Many readers of Acts today have a mistaken assumption: that the earliest believers "had it all together," in contrast to ourselves. There is a familiar hymn whose second verse begins this way: "if you cannot preach like Peter, if you cannot pray like Paul . . . ." The hymn implies Peter and Paul—and other church leaders like them—were faith superheroes.

But that is far from true. In Acts, the apostles are flawed human beings, slow to get on board with the Spirit's leading. Peter and Paul, the story's most prominent leaders, require forceful persuasion to enter critical events of their ministries. Peter, for example, embraces gentiles as full-fledged community members only after several persistent prods of the Holy Spirit (10:1—11:18).[22] Paul, likewise, requires a divine encounter with the risen Jesus to redirect him entirely from being a persecutor of the faith to a leading advocate (9:1-19). The narrative recounts Paul's experience at length three times, which only reiterates how blind such leaders have been and may be in relation to God's purposes.[23] In short, the apostles in Acts are flawed, fragile, imperfect people trying to keep up with the activity of the Holy Spirit. Acts is not a story about apostolic heroism. It is a story about a God who persists in calling flawed human beings to be witnesses.

---

20. Fitzmyer, *Acts*, 204.

21. González, *Story Luke Tells*, 120.

22. Peter testifies to gentiles because God compels him (Acts 10:9-16, 19-20, 28; cf. 10:44-48; 11:17), and the church embraces gentiles as full participants because miraculous events constrain it to do so (11:1-18; 15:12-19). Compare the conclusions of the apostolic council in 15:1-35, where refusing to embrace uncircumcised gentiles would constitute, in Peter's estimation, putting God to the test (15:10; cf. 11:19-24).

23. Acts 9:1-19; 22:1-21; 26:2-23. The third reiteration includes the proverb from Euripides ("It bodes ill for you to kick against the goads," *Bacchae* 795, Acts 26:14), which throughout Greek tragedy marks the folly of human beings who try to resist the gods (see Euripides, *Iphigenia in Tauris*, 1396; Pindar, *Pythian* 2.94-96; Aeschylus, *Agamemnon*, 1624; also *Psalms of Solomon* 16.4; Philo, *On the Decalogue*, 87).

Here is good news: according to Acts, being Jesus' witnesses requires nothing extraordinary. Jesus has no preliminary exams or prerequisites to gauge people's worthiness to be witnesses. If anything, his call banks upon imperfections that make their testimonies distinctive, personal, and colorful. For example, as Paul bears witness in Acts, he often retells his experience of being rerouted by Jesus (22:3–21; 26:4–23). This was neither honorable nor glamorous to retell. By first-century Roman cultural norms, it portrays Paul as weak, lacking control, and unmanly.[24] But his folly and humiliation shift focus to the saving work of Jesus in Paul's life and the genuineness of his change.

Wounded Witnesses

Faithful witness is holistic witness. As such, it does not hide our struggles and hardships under a veneer covering, nor is it disassociated from our pain and suffering. In fact, faithful testimony more often appreciates hardships as places where God has been distinctively present and faithful. In Acts, Paul talks about his experiences of unjust treatment as not only compatible but complementary to his witness about Jesus (26:4–8; 28:17–20; see also 16:37; 20:18–21, 31, 34–35; 24:12–21). The line between Paul's experience of the gospel and experience of difficulty is blurry, since the latter is related to and partially an outgrowth of the former, at least in Acts. Paul's testimony embraces a wide range of experiences he has had with the gospel and with serving as a leading witness of it.

Keri Day talks about the power of testifying about persistence through challenges, especially for those who identify as African American and live and work in racist environments. In her experiences of church communities faced with such challenges, "testifying was a way of showing we had overcome those things that attempted to assault and destroy our minds and even ability to hope."[25] In these contexts, "testifying was about bearing witness to a God who could heal in the midst of brokenness and help us face the truth of who we were and could be, if only we could participate in the loving work of the Spirit."[26] While as a white male I cannot profess to know firsthand the experiences of which Keri Day speaks, her spotlight on testimony practices among African American churches is an instructive

---

24. On this, see B. Wilson, *Unmanly Men*, 153–89.
25. Day, "Collective Act," 19.
26. Day, *Notes*, 2.

and insightful example of the biblical practice of bearing witness to God's faithfulness through trial and challenge.

As seen in Acts, faithful witness in Jesus' name needs to be authentic to ourselves, our experiences, our scars, and the messiness of our journeys. It needs to be true to who we are, where we have come from, and who we are called to be. In fact, our witness often gains credibility insofar as it reflects our warts, flaws, and imperfections.

In his book *The Wounded Healer*, Henri Nouwen suggests ministry is not grounded in a story that fixes or takes away our pain. Instead, ministry takes shape through acknowledging our mortality and brokenness within community.

> A Christian community is therefore a healing community not because wounds are cured and pains are alleviated, but because wounds and pains become openings or occasions for a new vision ... not as a stifling form of self-complaint, but as a recognition of God's saving promise.[27]

Nouwen's idea implies the vitality and importance of acknowledging our shortcomings and brokenness as part of our witness in Jesus' name. We testify to the good news of Jesus as a broken and wounded people. For people like us, the message of Jesus is good news, because it tells of a God who saves and stands with us in our brokenness, as seen especially in the cross of Christ.

Faithful witness is not an act of cover-up. It does not sugarcoat an otherwise rough and uncultivated subject. It is an act of testifying to the truth of how the gospel has intersected with our lives, however messy and difficult and challenging this life has been.

First Steps: Embracing the Story

Many people have the assumption that, to engage in faithful witness, they first need to learn more about the Bible and theology. Based on the stories of Luke and Acts, I think a more important starting place is what we have known and experienced of Jesus in our own lives. Bearing witness to anything assumes firsthand experience. It assumes we can speak to what we have seen, heard, and known. It neither assumes nor

---

27. Nouwen, *Wounded Healer*, 65–66.

requires extraordinary knowledge on our part. It simply assumes we can speak truthfully to our experience.

Given this, the starting place for faithful witness may not be formal study, but honest reflection—about our experiences of God, Jesus Christ, and the Holy Spirit. This does not require formal degrees or education. It requires taking stock of our experiences of faith and spirituality. This kind of reflection happens through addressing questions like these:

- Consider the story of your spiritual journey from childhood to today. What are the most significant moments along the way?
- Can you identify specific times in your life when you sensed God leading you?
- How have you grown or developed spiritually over the course of your life?
- Where have you experienced God in your life?
- How do you discern the presence of God in your life?
- Where or when have you encountered the living Christ?
- How has Christ saved, redeemed, or liberated you?
- How have you experienced or encountered Christ in community?
- How have you seen or sensed the Holy Spirit at work in your life?
- Where do you see the Holy Spirit at work in our world?
- What does it mean for you to trust or believe in God?
- What is most important to you about your faith?
- How is your life different because of your faith?
- Why is the gospel of Jesus Christ good news for you?
- Where do you sense God at work and leading you now?
- How do you sense God compelling you in community to work for justice for others?

These questions are not academically rigorous. They simply ask what difference the gospel of Jesus Christ has made in our lives. They invite us to reflect and speak to the ways we have known God's presence and work—and the tangible differences that has made.

Questions like these explore how our life journeys and faith intersect. They are questions more of spiritual direction than of biblical knowledge.

They ask how and where God's Spirit has been present in our lives to guide, lead, prod, and direct. Spiritual direction, after all, invests in asking what Henri Nouwen calls "the big questions, the fundamental questions, the universal ones."[28] Such questions are about where and how we have sensed God's presence in our lives. In asking such questions, we become more aware of how often and how deeply our own stories intersect with God's redeeming work in the world.

The title of this chapter is "Embracing the Story." The "story" being referenced is a hybrid story. First, it is the story of Jesus. It is a story of good news about God's saving activity among and for all creation. This story is the gospel (= good news) of Jesus Christ.

But we cannot know and understand this story apart from our lived experiences. The story of Jesus cannot be good news for us in the abstract, without connecting to our lives and circumstances. Good news, after all, can only be good when it is good *for you*.

This leads to the second aspect of the story: the ways in which the story of Jesus intersects with and shapes our own story. Like all people, we make sense of the story of Jesus from the vantage point of our own stories. Our life experiences create an interpretive lens through which we experience and know the message of Jesus as good news for us. The story of Jesus as we understand it is not just a story about who Jesus is and what he has done—it is also a story about what he has done *for us*. Although the story's focus is Jesus and his activity, our lived experiences are the lens through which we understand the primary story's personal and ultimate significance.

I do not mean to suggest "the story" to which we bear witness is more about ourselves than about Jesus. Far from it! Were it not for the story of Jesus and its impact on our lives, we would have no story of good news to share. Instead, the story at the center of our faithful witness is the story of Jesus (= the first aspect), but from the vantage point of how it has changed and impacted our lives (= the second aspect). The story we embrace is about Jesus, but from the perspective of how we have known it and been transformed by it.

Conclusion

Like his earliest followers, Jesus calls us his witnesses and invites us into the practice of bearing witness. The good news is we do not need to be

---

28. Nouwen, *Spiritual Direction*, 5.

extraordinary people with extraordinary stories or extraordinary achievements. Jesus does not call those who are equipped. He equips those who are called.

What faithful witness requires most of all is authenticity to who we are. It needs to be real to our stories, our experiences, and our journeys. It needs to be authentic to who we are. To this end, faithful witness begins with a look in the mirror. It begins with a long, hard look at our journeys and how God has been faithful throughout. It involves taking stock of the work of God in our lives, so that we may speak to God's saving work firsthand.

A friend of mine used to struggle a great deal with her faith story. She grew up in a context where people associated Christian testimony with stories of dramatic change—extraordinary experiences that changed the courses of people's lives overnight. But my friend had no dramatic events to share. She had been baptized as an infant, raised by a faithful family, nurtured by a grace-centered church, and taught the faith from day one. In comparison to the life-changing events told by others, her journey seemed boring. Although grateful her faith had been such a constant in her life, it seemed like those who visited the extremes of rock bottom valleys and spiritual mountaintops had more interesting stories for others to hear.

That was before she had a spiritual awakening—not a conversion or dramatic change, but a basic realization: God has been present and active throughout her life. Even more, God has been no less present and active in her life than anyone else's.

However laughably simple, this realization was a watershed moment for my friend. The context in which she grew up had so emphasized and applauded the dramatic and the extraordinary that she had overlooked the value of her own story, undramatic as it may be. Hers was a story of God's ongoing faithfulness in her life, in ways that were real, distinctive, and worth hearing.

I share my friend's story not to elevate hers above others', but to offer her realization for you and me: God has been richly present and active throughout your life, no matter its course. We are invited to explore and discern the places and ways God has shown up, whether obvious or not, to gain a clearer sense of how our stories are sacred journeys directed by God in Christ through the Holy Spirit.

The Christian life, after all, is a journey. As Marcus Borg points out, a journey is a process that involves our whole being. It involves our feet as well as our minds and our heads. A journey involves following a path or a way. To be on a journey is not to be involved in aimless wandering, though there may be times when it feels like that. . . . [T]he Christian life is more like following a path than it is about believing things with our minds.[29]

The call of Jesus to be his witnesses extends to you and me today. And the first step is simply to embrace the story of Jesus and how it has changed, impacted, and influenced our own stories. This helps us see more clearly how the gospel is good news, not in the abstract, but in tangible ways for you and me today.

Questions for Discussion

1. Under the section "What Witnesses Do," the chapter emphasizes how Jesus did not call his followers "'preachers,' 'proclaimers,' 'spokespeople,' or 'heralds.' Nor does he call them 'ambassadors,' 'prophets,' or 'priests.'" What do you like (or not like) about the language "witness" in comparison to these options?

2. The chapter suggests faithful witness involves not just the story of Jesus but also the ways it has affected and intersected with our lives. What do you think of this?

3. Under the section "Wounded Witnesses," the chapter suggests faithful witness "needs to be authentic to ourselves, our experiences, our scars, and the messiness of our journeys. It needs to be true to who we are, where we have come from, and who we are called to be." What are some examples of messiness or scars in your own testimony? How do these experiences inform or enrich your testimony?

4. Consider the questions listed under "First Steps: Embracing the Story." Pick a few questions to address. If possible, discuss them with others.

5. The chapter concludes by emphasizing that Jesus' call to be his witnesses extends to us today. How often do you think about this as you approach your daily life and faith?

---

29. Borg, "Faith: A Journey of Trust."

Resources for Further Exploration

- Bauer, David R. *The Book of Acts as Story: A Narrative-Critical Study*. Grand Rapids: Baker, 2021.
- Day, Keri. *Notes of a Native Daughter: Testifying in Theological Education*. Grand Rapids: Eerdmans, 2021.
- Marshall, I. Howard, and David Peterson, editors. *Witness to the Gospel: The Theology of Acts*. Grand Rapids: Eerdmans, 1998.
- Moloney, Francis J. *Witnesses to the Ends of the Earth: New Testament Reflections on Mission*. Mahwah, NJ: Paulist, 2022.
- Nouwen, Henri J. M., with Michael J. Christensen and Rebecca J. Laird. *Spiritual Direction: Wisdom for the Long Walk of Faith*. San Francisco: HarperOne, 2006.
- Nouwen, Henri J. M. *The Wounded Healer: Ministry in Contemporary Society*. New York: Image, 2013.

Action Steps for Further Consideration

- Read through Acts, paying special attention to the ways followers of Jesus are called to bear witness in different places and spaces. Don't focus simply on the speeches. Notice also how the message is shared through acts of hospitality, generosity, assistance, and advocacy.
- Write down a synopsis of your spiritual journey, from childhood to today. How has God been present, active, and an engaged partner throughout your journey? Share with a trusted friend.
- In some contexts, people bear witness to events and experiences which they cannot deny. They attest to things whose truthfulness is clear to them. Considering your spiritual journey, what are some critical experiences, divine encounters, or watershed moments that you cannot deny from your own journey of faith?
- Consider the ways words and phrases like witness, bearing witness, and testimony are used today. How do these uses inform, enhance, or challenge your sense of the call of Jesus to be his witnesses in Scripture?

2

Telling the Story

> While many church members sing "I Love to Tell the Story," the sad truth is that too few do.
>
> —J. Brent Bill[1]

OVER TWENTY YEARS AGO, the then-presiding bishop of the ELCA Mark Hansen lamented: "It's been said that the average Lutheran invites someone to worship once every twenty-three years. If that's not bad enough, research shows that it takes three invitations before the people invited come."[2] David Daubert followed this up with an observation of his own: "Since it's easier to invite someone to church than to tell someone what trusting Christ means to me, I don't even want to guess how infrequently we talk to others about Jesus."[3]

Although these comments pertain to Lutherans, it is not just Lutherans who resonate with these experiences. However anecdotal, they reflect traits of many people of Christian faith today.

This is not merely a character flaw. There are good reasons for hesitancy, sensitivity, and sometimes even silence when it comes to telling others about our faith. But excelling at silence all the time only implies the

---

1. Quoted in L. Daniel, *Tell It Like It Is*, ii.
2. Hanson, *Faithful Yet Changing*, 43.
3. Daubert, "Cure for Lutheran Laryngitis?"

opposite message: this faith must not entail any good news—or it must not be for everyone.

Acts tells a different tale. In the kickoff story of Acts, the result of the Holy Spirit's arrival is *speaking* the message of Jesus. At Pentecost, the Spirit enables followers of Jesus to declare verbally (and miraculously) God's "wondrous deeds of power" in many languages, so that the widest array of hearers might understand. The Holy Spirit arrives to make faithful witness in Jesus' name happen—and at Pentecost it's by way of a publicly spoken word. In response, those empowered cannot be silent.

What does this mean for faithful witness today? Let us consider the story of Pentecost more closely.

Pentecost: Acts 2:1-41

As discussed in chapter 1, the opening scene of Acts sets the stage for empowering people to bear witness in Jesus' name. Like Luke 1-2, Acts 1 serves as a preface to the larger narrative, highlighting significant events to come.

Right after this, Acts 2 kicks off the narrative with its first major event. Like Jesus' inaugural address in the opening chapters of Luke's Gospel (4:16-30), Pentecost is the inaugural event of Acts. By a dramatic appearance of the Holy Spirit, the community of Jesus' followers is empowered and commissioned to speak in other languages. Different from other occasions in the New Testament of speaking in tongues (glossolalia), where inspired speech is unintelligible to most hearers, here at Pentecost people use existing human languages, allowing the most people to hear and understand.[4]

> 1 When the day of Pentecost had come, they were all together in one place. 2 And suddenly from heaven there came a sound like the rush of a violent wind, and it filled the entire house where they were sitting. 3 Divided tongues, as of fire, appeared among them, and a tongue rested on each of them. 4 All of them were filled with the Holy Spirit and began to speak in other languages, as the Spirit gave them ability.
>
> 5 Now there were devout Jews from every people under heaven living in Jerusalem. 6 And at this sound the crowd gathered and was bewildered, because each one heard them speaking

---

4. Cf. 1 Corinthians 14:2, 9, 13-19. So Fitzmyer, *Acts*, 239; C. K. Barrett, *Acts*, 1:109. While Keener appreciates the distinction, he does not endorse it rigidly since he finds all forms of Spirit-inspired speech in the New Testament as serving the purpose of cross-cultural communication (*Acts*, 1:804-31).

in the native language of each. 7 Amazed and astonished, they asked, "Are not all these who are speaking Galileans? 8 And how is it that we hear, each of us, in our own native language? 9 Parthians, Medes, Elamites, and residents of Mesopotamia, Judea and Cappadocia, Pontus and Asia, 10 Phrygia and Pamphylia, Egypt and the parts of Libya belonging to Cyrene, and visitors from Rome, both Jews and proselytes, 11 Cretans and Arabs—in our own languages we hear them speaking about God's deeds of power." 12 All were amazed and perplexed, saying to one another, "What does this mean?" (Acts 2:1–12)

Pentecost has a long history before this event in Acts. In the Torah, it is a harvest feast called the Feast of Weeks.[5] It started as a day celebrating the first gatherings of the wheat harvest (Exod 34:22). Soon enough, it became identified with a feast at the *end* of harvest. In time, the festival became associated with the giving of the covenant at Sinai and the issuing of the Torah to Moses.[6] The name "Pentecost"—from the Greek word "fiftieth" (*pentēkostos*)—is what Greek-speaking Jews called the Feast of Weeks, since it took place fifty days after the Passover.

By the first century, many Jews celebrated Pentecost by pilgrimage to Jerusalem.[7] At this time, many more Jews lived outside Palestine than within, since for centuries they had emigrated to surrounding regions for various reasons. In an era where travel was more cumbersome and difficult, many immigrants made pilgrimage to Jerusalem first for the Passover (fifty days earlier) and remained there through Pentecost. Other Jews from diaspora regions came to reside in Jerusalem for economic or other reasons, settling there late in life.[8] Whether the audience at Pentecost is predominately visitors on pilgrimage, or residents originating from elsewhere, is not clear.[9] What is clear is how the gathered audience reflects a diversity of people from across the world.

---

5. Exod 23:16; 34:22; Lev 23:15–21; Deut 16:9–10, 16. In the New Testament, Paul uses "first fruits" language (Greek *aparchē*) for first installments of forthcoming things: Rom 8:23; 11:16; 16:5; 1 Cor 15:20; 16:15; see also 2 Thess 2:13; Jas 1:18; Rev 14:4.

6. *Jubilees* 1:1; 6:17–19; 14:20; 1 QS 1:8—2:25. Fitzmyer, *Acts*, 233–37.

7. So the first-century Jewish historian Josephus, who refers to celebrating Pentecost as "the Feast of Assembly" (*Antiquities* 3.10.6 §252; cf. *Jewish War* 6.5.3 §299).

8. Gaventa, *Acts*, 75.

9. The verb in Acts 2:5 for "living" in Jerusalem (*katoikountes*) may mean "sojourning" (so Fitzmyer, *Acts*, 231), but more often in Luke-Acts it signifies something along the lines of permanent residence (Luke 11:26; Acts 1:220; 7:2, 4, 48; 17:24, 25). The ambiguity suggests Luke did not care to distinguish rigidly between residents and visitors.

Telling the Story

The story's list of regions, nations, and cities is a curious one. First, it lists some people groups that once were nations, but at this point are scattered among regions ruled by others (Parthians, Medes, Elamites). Second, it surprisingly omits places in the eastern Mediterranean mentioned elsewhere in Acts, from which Jewish pilgrims might likely have come to Jerusalem: Achaia, Macedonia, Cilicia, Syria, and Galatia. What guides the selection and ordering of the list seems to be the four compass points, with Judea (Jerusalem) as an anchor point at the center:

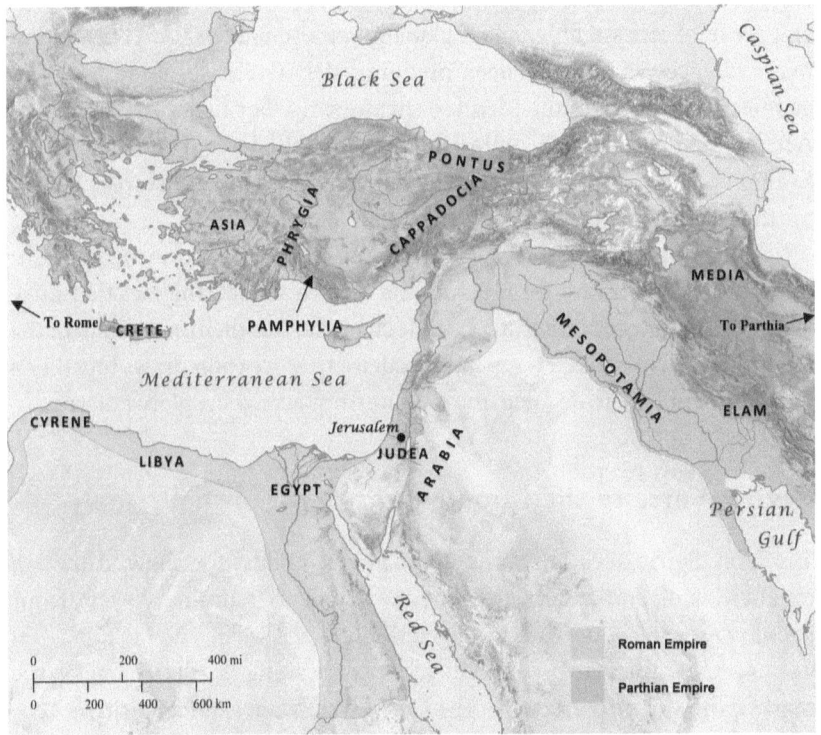

Nations at Pentecost, Biblemapper Atlas (biblemapper.com),
copyright 2023 David P. Barrett, used with permission

Northeast: Parthians, Medes, Elamites, and Mesopotamia (2:9)
At the center: Judea (2:9)
Northwest: Cappadocia, Pontus and Asia, Phrygia and Pamphylia (2:9)

Instead, he envisions all of them as part of the miraculous outpouring of the Spirit that prefigures worldwide witness (so Keener, *Acts*, 1:833–35).

Southwest and West: Egypt, Libya, Cyrene, Rome, and Crete (2:10–11a)
Southeast: Arabia (Arabs) (2:11)

In order of appearance, the list moves from northeast to northwest (via Judea) to southwest/west to southeast. The only city is Rome, which is likely named due to its strong connections to Jerusalem (for trade and travel), its significance for Acts, and its geopolitical importance for Christians in the first century.

Of course, this list does not actually reflect "every nation under heaven," as Luke boasts (Acts 2:5). His language uses hyperbole to give the general sense of an assembly that is globally representative.[10] After all, Luke's first audiences would have been predominately Greek-speaking Jews and gentiles somewhere in the Mediterranean world. For them, the nations in Acts 2 would have broadly represented the inhabited world known to them. Even if not globally representative by our standards, Luke's list was likely so for the first hearers of Acts.

The audience at Pentecost, then, is an extensive and inclusive gathering of Jewish faithful from across the known world. The fact that Luke labels them "devout" (*eulabeis*) further characterizes them as a group of the committed.[11] No ordinary day in Jerusalem, this occasion draws together a distillation of Israel's devoted and devout from across the global diaspora.

Giving Voice to the Good News

The Holy Spirit does not show up at Pentecost just for show. Although tongues "as of fire" appear, the purpose of this extraordinary event is for people to speak about God's saving activity.

As C. K. Barrett points out, in Acts speaking is "the characteristic mark of the Spirit's presence."[12] The Holy Spirit is not a quiet Spirit. In Acts, when the Spirit fills, leads, or empowers people, it typically results in a spoken word. Although many Christians associate Jesus with "the Word" due

---

10. Other ancient authors do similarly. For example, Pseudo-Callisthenes provides a list of ten nations gathered in hostility against Alexander, plus "all the other great nations of the East" (*Alexander* 1.2). On possible sources for Luke's list of nations (e.g., Gen 10, zodiacal lists), see Bauckham, "James," 417–27; Keener, *Acts*, 1:833–44.

11. Within the New Testament, the word *eulabēs* means "devout, reverent, faithful." Elsewhere, it often means "careful, cautious," especially in managing political change or overseeing others. Diggle et al., *Cambridge Greek Lexicon*, 1:621.

12. C. K. Barrett, *Acts*, 2:lxxxiv.

to language in John's Gospel, the activity of the Holy Spirit in Acts justifies a similarly strong association between God's word and the *Spirit* of God. In this narrative, the Holy Spirit will not remain silent. The Spirit speaks regularly, prophetically, and boldly. And where the Spirit of God speaks, the potential for transformative change is high.

Further, the Holy Spirit's speaking is not a performance for its own sake. The end goal is not simply a prophetic word to be marveled at. God's Spirit speaks so that *people may hear*.[13] The prophetic word is not only communicative; it is relational. It speaks to, for, and among human beings. The real wonder of Pentecost is not that Jesus' followers speak in public spaces, but that others can hear and understand their words. As Justo González notes: "the purpose of the outpouring of the Spirit is not to know the hidden secrets of God, but rather to give witness to Jesus."[14]

Twice the story emphasizes—each time with dual verb pairings—how "amazed" (or "astounded"), "in awe," and "perplexed" the audience is (2:7, 12).[15] The precise reason for their amazement is voiced in the question: "And how is it that we hear, each of us, in our own native language?" (v. 8). At a loss for an answer, they ask simply: "What does this mean?" (v. 12).

What is most extraordinary about the Pentecost event is how the Holy Spirit enables people to speak in many, diverse languages. This is quite a contrast to what would have been an alternative strategy: to unite all voices into a common language. This approach would have been simpler, less complicated, and by most standards easier. But it would also have conveyed an implicit, negative message about the diversity of languages and cultures at the assembly. It would have suggested they are dispensable and worth removing in the name of uniformity.

However, that is not what the Holy Spirit does. Easier as that might have been, the Spirit instead blesses a path of diversity, not uniformity. As Eric Barreto puts it: "At Pentecost, God makes a clear choice. God joins us in the midst of the messiness and the difficulties of speaking different languages, eating different foods, and living in different cultures. That is good news indeed."[16]

---

13. Keener observes: "Luke's primary concern is not simply prophetic speech in general but especially prophetic speech that extends to other peoples" (*Acts*, 1:824).

14. González, *Story Luke Tells*, 120.

15. *Existanto* (vv. 7, 12): "amazed" or "astounded" (lit. "stood outside [themselves]"); *ethaumazon* (v. 7): "marveled" or "were in awe"; *diēporoun* (v. 12): "perplexed" or "were at a loss."

16. Barreto, "What Happened at Pentecost?"

Willie James Jennings point out: "To learn a language requires submission to a people."[17] At Pentecost, that's what the Spirit of God compels Jesus' followers to do. They are led not to coerce others into a particular pattern, but to enter their cultural worlds and to speak the gospel in their languages. If at Pentecost the Holy Spirit had simply enabled the hearers to understand the language of the apostles, it would have given the apostles a measure of control. Justo González points out:

> If the Spirit decided that all were to understand the language of the disciples, the inevitable consequence would be that from that time on, the language, culture, and customs of the disciples would be normative in the life of the church. In order to be a leader in that church, it would be necessary to speak the tongue of the disciples, who therefore would also remain in control.[18]

In Acts, the Spirit of God neither fosters nor condones controlling tendencies among Jesus' followers. This is a significant point to ponder. Instead, the Spirit compels them to relinquish control—over others, over conventional community boundaries, over their notions of orthodoxy, and over their lives. Throughout Acts, the Holy Spirit forces people outside their comfort zones to welcome and receive others more fully and genuinely in Jesus' name. In this way, the Spirit reflects the nature of a God whose scope of concern is organically global.[19]

At Pentecost, the Holy Spirit pushes followers of Jesus to speak a life-giving message to others—in ways that were new, uncomfortable, and cross-cultural. "It bears repeating," Willie James Jennings notes, "this is not what the disciples imagined or hoped would manifest the power of the Holy Spirit."[20] Although miraculously empowered by the Spirit, it was no small thing for these people simply to speak their message publicly for all to hear.

---

17. Jennings, *Acts*, 29.

18. González, *Story Luke Tells*, 120.

19. Jennings describes the message of Acts as one about a "God who seeks to place in each of us desire for those outside of us, outside our worlds of culture, clan, nation, tribe, faith, politics, class, and species" (*Acts*, 12).

20. Jennings, *Acts*, 29. He adds: "The gesture of speaking another language is born not of the desire of the disciples but of God."

The Power and Significance of Words

For many people who identify as Christian today, talking about faith is difficult. Talking about it *with others* is even more complicated and challenging.

There are many reasons why. In the United States, matters of faith have often been associated with the realm of the private and personal, making it less readily a subject of conversation. A 2018 Barna study suggests the biggest reason US Christians are reluctant to talk about their faith today is a fear of provoking tensions, starting arguments, or introducing awkwardness to existing relationships.[21]

Indeed, many people today are increasingly afraid of coming across as overly aggressive or fundamentalist if they speak about their faith. Barna suggests millennials (born 1981–96) are much more likely than preceding generations to fear being identified as intolerant or narrow-minded. Since millennials have grown up in an increasingly pluralistic society, with many friends and acquaintances different from themselves, they are more sensitive to offending others and to forms of religious intolerance associated with more fundamentalist groups.[22]

This concern is not unfounded. Many people have had painful experiences with certain forms of Christianity, making any words about the faith ring entirely hollow (or even harmful) without first acknowledging and taking seriously their experiences. In my years as a pastor and professor, I have known many people who have spent years of their lives feeling barred from church due to their marriage status, sexuality, or gender identity—or that of their children. Still others carry scars from experiences of Christians who have been more passionate about preserving the status quo than about advocating for just laws and civil liberties for all people of every race. These experiences are not quickly forgotten. These considerations invite Christians of all kinds to pause and listen before speaking brashly. Christianity, after all, has historically engaged in harmful practices when its work has been wedded (often unwittingly) to interests and practices of control, manipulation, or exploitation.

At Pentecost, strategies of control are not what the Spirit is up to. In this story and throughout Acts, we find a Holy Spirit who dissolves traditional

---

21. At 28 percent of respondents (Barna, "Why People"). The second biggest reason was "I don't feel like I know enough" (at 17 percent).

22. Barna, "Why People." The percentage of millennials who carry this fear is not necessarily high (10 percent), but is demonstrably higher than all prior generations (3 percent for Generation X, 4 percent for boomers, and 1 percent for elders).

barriers, who compels apostles and church leaders to speak in new ways, and who ignites into existence a church that is more chaotically diverse than conventionally controllable. The story of Pentecost—an event often identified as the "birthday of the church"—is not a story of order and control, but one of an unpredictable Holy Spirit who suddenly shows up and sets a global movement ablaze in a very messy, organic, and diversified way.

At the same time, the story of Pentecost is an event centered around spoken words. The primary result of the Spirit's arrival is to enable audible, public, intelligible, spoken words about God's saving activity to others. And not just to close friends and acquaintances. But to strangers, visitors, and immigrants; to people outside our social circles; to people who do not share our assumptions and values; and to people who do not think and act like we do. At Pentecost and throughout Acts, the Holy Spirit is not a silent spirit.

How, then, does the Holy Spirit call followers of Jesus to speak the good news of Jesus today?

Although faithful witness can happen in many and diverse ways, talking about it with others in a nonconfrontational, non-condemning, sensitive, and invitational way has often been one of the most effective. Speaking about our faith introduces the topic explicitly, shows that it matters to us personally, and ideally opens a door for conversation. Talking starts a dialogue, creating opportunities for good things.

To be clear: talking about the faith is not the same thing as more aggressive approaches like door-to-door cold calls, pointed questions about eternity, or bait and switch strategies—things John Bowen associates with "flasher evangelism."[23] Talking about the faith can simply mean talking about things variously associated with it, like mentioning a daily faith practice, talking about a church community, voicing gratefulness to God for something, offering to pray for someone, leading a table grace, mentioning a church food justice ministry, or explaining how our faith informs our convictions about something. This kind of talking about faith need not be foreign to who we are or intrusive to our relationships. It's the kind of thing human beings normally do when our lives have been changed by something good.

---

23. Bowen, *Evangelism for "Normal" People*, 19. He borrows the idea from Margaret Atwood, who in the story "The Scarlet Ibis" compares "religious people" (i.e., evangelistic people) to flashers who "made her nervous" because "you would be going along with them in the normal way, and then there could be a swift movement" of change to something that felt inappropriate and dehumanizing.

Telling the Story

Dave Daubert has passion for invitational evangelism because his own life was changed by it. He was not raised in a church. But as a college student, he had two friends ("Scott" and "John") who were devout Roman Catholics. Regularly on late Saturday afternoons, they stopped what they were doing to go to mass (worship). And nearly every week, they invited Daubert: "Do you want to come too?" Although he declined for months, one day he decided to go. It became instrumental to changing Daubert's life.[24] Scott and John never did say much. But what they did was enough.

Talking about faith inevitably entails risks—of tension, awkwardness, and missteps. That's because unlike mundane topics like the weather, faith lays claim to deeply important things: about God, life and death, good and evil, ethical living, care for the world, and our purpose in life. Simply to profess a faith in God automatically entails a distinctive interpretation of these weighty things. We can hardly expect everyone to agree. In fact, in a society where attention is often given to the most outspoken and provocative voices, people of faith may less so expect warm reception from others. The risks of tension, apathy, and misunderstanding rightly invite people of faith to proceed with great care.

However, people of nearly every generation, cultural background, economic status, and educational training have questions about life's meaning and purpose. Almost universally, human beings long for a sense that their life matters, that their work matters, and that there is more to life than simply breathing and dying.

Take Ali, for example. At ten years old, she was diagnosed with an aggressive form of leukemia. From then on, life became very different for her. But as she fought leukemia, someone invited her to a cancer support group hosted at our church. Ali came, experienced a caring community, and there encountered a gracious God. Although not raised in the church, she wanted to be baptized and to take communion for the first time. Just over a month later, Ali passed away from cancer, but not before throwing the biggest cancer fundraising party the city had seen, raising $14,000 to assist young people who would fight cancer after her. Especially in her final weeks, she lived with a clear sense of purpose, freedom, and life, attesting to the beauty of the gospel and its impact on a particular young person's life.

---

24. Daubert, "Evangelism 101."

A Gift of the Spirit

Many people of Christian faith find it hard to talk about or even mention their faith. The good news of Pentecost is this: *the Holy Spirit will help us do so.*

Many people mistakenly assume too much responsibility when it comes to talking about faith, as if the results are entirely in their control. On this point, some people read the story of Pentecost with an unhelpful focus on the results: an extraordinary number of "about three thousand" respond favorably to Peter's message (Acts 2:41). For one, Luke's numerical estimate probably exaggerates, by our standards.[25] For another, this response is extraordinary (i.e., miraculous), unparalleled elsewhere in Acts and in history. The miraculous response at Pentecost is not a blueprint for reproduction today, but a testament to the incredible work of the Holy Spirit at the very beginnings of the church.

In talking about our faith, it is not our job to convert people or to make them believe. We do not have control over how faith takes shape in others. That is God's work. Faith is up to the Holy Spirit to create within people. If we believe faith is ultimately a gift of the Spirit (Gal 5:22–23), then it is not ours to make or produce. It is ours to scatter and sow seeds of the gospel, leaving the growth to God (Mark 4:1–9, 13–20; 1 Cor 3:5–9).[26] We are called simply to bear faithful witness to the gospel in word and deed, letting the Holy Spirit do the rest.

I had a high school classmate named "Evan." In our later years of high school, when I became excited about my faith, he took notice. He often teased me: "So what has God revealed to you today?" "How would you rate the holiness of your class on a scale of one to ten?" "You should preach a sermon on the front lawn after school—it would save people from hell." Although not mean spirited, he meant to poke fun. I tried not to take it personally.

Nearly a decade later, to my surprise, Evan reached out. He told me about an experience that became a wake-up to God's work in his life. Most surprisingly, he credited my words and example as planting some of the first seeds. He wanted to reach out to tell me. I have no memory of anything profound or constructive that I ever said to Evan. At that time, I was far more

---

25. Dunn, *Acts*, 34.

26. The parable of the sower (Mark 4:1–9, 13–20) also appears in Matthew 13:1–9, 18–23, and Luke 8:4–8, 11–15.

focused on figuring out my own stuff. But somehow the Holy Spirit used the opportunity to plant something that would grow beautiful years later.

In Scripture, the Holy Spirit gives people words to speak at the times they most need it. This is true not just at extraordinary events like Pentecost, but also at other times. Jesus tells his followers: "do not worry about how you are to defend yourselves or what you are to say; for the Holy Spirit will teach you at that very hour what you ought to say" (Luke 12:11b–12). When human words fail, the Holy Spirit will not remain silent. Whatever the result, followers of Jesus are promised they will be neither alone nor without words in times of trial.[27]

First Steps: Sharing Testimony

Talking about faith benefits from a little practice. If we want to talk about God on weekdays, we should first learn to talk about God on Sundays. If we want to talk about God in our daily lives, we might start by talking about God at church. One historic practice for doing this is the sharing of testimony.

Sharing testimony about one's lived experience of the faith is an established practice especially prominent in African American, Methodist, Quaker (Society of Friends), and Evangelical and free church traditions.[28] Testimony may refer narrowly to sharing the story of how one came to faith, but more often it refers broadly to sharing about any event or experience that attests to the work of God in a Christian's life. Testimonies are often shared in the context of worship services, but also at evangelistic events, in podcasts, and in written and online publications. Practices of sharing testimony are not nearly as common in mainline, Euro-American Christian churches. In these traditions, worshipers participate more often through crafted liturgy. A downside to this is a lack of opportunity and encouragement for more unscripted forms of faith talk.

Lillian Daniel is a pastor who strove to revive the practice of testimony in a congregation of "reserved protestant New Englanders"—the Church of the Redeemer (United Church of Christ) in New Haven, Connecticut. Since she sensed a hunger in her people for constructive ways to talk about their faith, Daniel decided to explore ways to bring a historic practice like testimony back:

---

27. In addition to Luke 12:11–12, see Mark 13:11; Matt 10:19–20; John 14:26; Luke 21:14–15; Acts 4:1–22 (esp. v. 8). In Acts, see 4:1–22 (esp. v. 8); 6:8—8:1a (esp. 7:55).

28. Practices of testimony are also prevalent in Mormonism and Islam.

> Despite the historical recordings of testimony, for the most part, testimony does not thrive as a practice in my denomination anymore. Today it is more a practice of the free church tradition, or evangelicalism. . . . Testimony is not traditionally a practice that we associate with justice-seeking churches. Testimony has become a practice that makes us think of one individual speaking about a relationship with a personal savior. But in rediscovering this practice in a mainline church, and recovering its history, I saw that we bring our ecclesiology to the practice.[29]

In embarking on this initiative, Daniel made modifications (e.g., calling them "reflections"), set some ground rules (e.g., all testimonies needed to name God), and gave a time frame (Lenten worship services). Then she invited people to do it.

The result was transformational on many levels. It strengthened bonds within their community; it fostered more careful consideration of and reflection about people's faith practices; and it "drew us closer to God as individuals and as a community."[30]

> God's grace broke in through the words of us ordinary people all the time. We came to know one another and God with a sharpness I could never have imagined in community. Often I was called back once again to the beautiful vision of the church that had made me want to serve it full time. Over and over, a generous God shined through in words about dolls, ties, committees, old churches, and new ones. A practice that at first seemed borrowed from other traditions or plucked artificially from a history long passed now belonged to us at Church of the Redeemer.[31]

As Lillian Daniel's experience shows, the practice of testimony is more than a spotlight on individualistic faith and personal experience. It brings the personal into communal spaces, making it ultimately a shared community experience.

Thomas Hoyt Jr. similarly draws attention to how communal the practice of testimony really is:

---

29. L. Daniel, *Tell It Like It Is*, xix. Elsewhere Daniel writes: "While no one would use the word *testimony*, based on what I saw happening at Church of the Redeemer, I sensed our congregation was hungry for the practice of testimony" (10, italics original).

30. L. Daniel, *Tell It Like It Is*, 13.

31. L. Daniel, *Tell It Like It Is*, 161–62.

> [Testimony] ties individuals to communities. Although only one person may be speaking at a time, that person's speech takes place within the context of other people's listening, expecting, and encouraging. In testimony, a believer describes what God has done in her life, in words both biblical and personal, and the hands of her friends clap in affirmation. Her individual speech thus becomes part of an affirmation that is shared.[32]

Hoyt describes testimony as "one of the most cherished practices of the Black Church," prevalent among African American church communities since their historic beginnings.[33] He points out the distinctive role testimony has played for oppressed and marginalized communities, as a practice that welcomes the sharing of life experiences, both trials and triumphs, in the context of a faith community that is safe. For oppressed communities, the practice of testimony bears witness not only to the redeeming work of God today, but also to the challenges of daily living in ways that are cathartic and healing.

Practices of testimony have different histories and significance across different church traditions. For example, as a white male, I do not know firsthand the distinctive experiences that African American church communities have derived from testimony practices. But in observing and honoring the significance it has had for other communities, we too may learn and consider ways to practice testimony faithfully in our own communities. However we go about it, the practice encourages us to use our words to attest to the good news and faithfulness of God in Christ in our lives and in the world today.

Conclusion: A Good News People

Throughout the New Testament, and especially in Luke and Acts, followers of Jesus are called to bear witness (or testify).[34] They bear witness not

---

32. Hoyt, "Testimony," 94.

33. Hoyt, "Testimony," 91 (quotation) and 95.

34. For example: Mark 1:44 (and parallels Matt 8:4; Luke 5:14); Mark 13:9 (parallel Matt 10:18); Matt 24:14; Luke 21:13; John 1:7–8, 15, 32, 34; 3:11, 26, 28; 19:35; 21:24; Acts 4:33; 14:3; 20:26; 22:18; 23:11; 26:22; 1 Cor 2:1; 15:151; John 1:2; 4:14; 5:9–10; Rev 1:2; 22:16, 18. See also Rom 10:2; 1 Cor 1:6; Acts 10:43; 13:22. The identification of Jesus' followers as "witnesses" is also relevant: Luke 24:48; Acts 1:8, 22; 2:32; 3:15; 5:32; 10:39, 41; 13:31; 22:15, 20; 26:16. On this word family and its use in the New Testament, see Strathmann, "μάρτυς, μαρτυρέω, μαρτυρία, μαρτύριον," 489–504.

only to the work of God in Christ but also to how they have experienced and known it firsthand. Most often they bear witness in ways that involve spoken words. Bearing witness in Acts especially takes shape through spoken words, inspired by a Holy Spirit who, more than anything else, enables people to give voice to the message.

Christians believe that the story of God's activity in the life, death, and resurrection of Jesus Christ is good news. Further, it is good news for everyone. And good news is exciting and natural to share.

Talking about this message and our faith is something the Holy Spirit invites us to do—and helps us to do it. It need not be dramatic, articulate, lengthy, or impressive. In fact, chances are high it would be better off none of those things. It needs simply to be authentic to who we are, genuine to our lived experience, and organic to our personalities. Talking about the faith, after all, is less something we are to "do" than it is to reflect who we are. In both word and deed, faithful witness attests to God's work in Jesus Christ in Scripture and in the world today.

In Scripture, the Holy Spirit gives people the words to say at the times they most need it. The same Holy Spirit is present with us today and is nearby to assist us with a faithful witness that our world most needs.

Questions for Discussion

1. Read the story of Pentecost (Acts 2:1–41) and consider the following questions:
   - Willie James Jennings points out that speaking in other languages "is not what the disciples imagined or hoped would manifest the power of the Holy Spirit."[35] What do you think the experience must have been like for them?
   - Notice the diversity of peoples gathered, the variety of languages presumably spoken, and the awe and wonder in response. What do you think this experience must have been like for those present?
   - Imagine if Pentecost had taken shape instead through a vision of the risen Jesus, through a unifying of people's languages, or through a recruitment strategy of the apostles. How different would that have been?

35. Jennings, *Acts*, 29.

- If the Pentecost story is fundamentally a story about the Holy Spirit, what does the story say?

2. C. K. Barrett points out that, in Acts, speaking is "the characteristic mark of the Spirit's presence."[36] In other words, the Spirit of God is not a quiet Spirit. More than anything else in Acts, the Holy Spirit enables and empowers speaking. How does this make you think about the Holy Spirit's work in our lives today?

3. Consider experiences you—or others—have had in trying to learn a new language. Now consider what the Spirit did at Pentecost. What does this suggest about the things God calls us to do today?

4. A major theme of the chapter is that the Holy Spirit is present to give followers of Jesus the words to say when they most need them. Consider times or experiences when you think the Holy Spirit gave you or someone you know the words to say at a time they were most needed. What was that experience like?

5. What experiences have you or others had with sharing testimony in a church community? What does this chapter prompt you to consider about the practice?

6. What are your greatest fears or concerns with talking about your faith with others? What would help you feel more interested or excited about it?

Resources for Further Exploration

- Barna. "Why People Are Reluctant to Discuss Faith." August 14, 2018. https://www.barna.com/research/reasons-for-reluctance/.
- Daniel, Lillian. *Tell It Like It Is: Reclaiming the Practice of Testimony*. Lanham, MD: Alban Institute, 2006. Especially the preface (xiii–xxiv) and introduction (1–14).
- González, Justo L. *The Story Luke Tells: Luke's Unique Witness to the Gospel*. Grand Rapids: Eerdmans, 2015. Chapter 8 (pp. 111–25).

---

36. C. K. Barrett, *Acts*, 2:lxxxiv.

- Hoyt, Thomas, Jr. "Testimony." In *Practicing Our Faith: A Way of Life for a Searching People*, edited by Dorothy C. Bass, 91–103. San Francisco: Jossey-Bass, 1997.
- Jennings, Willie James. *Acts*. Belief: A Theological Commentary on the Bible. Louisville: Westminster John Knox, 2017. Pp. 27–36.
- Long, Thomas G. *Testimony: Talking Ourselves into Being Christian*. Hoboken, NJ: Jossey-Bass, 2003.

Action Steps for Further Consideration

- Consult the Barna research article "Why People Are Reluctant to Discuss Faith." Do the reasons named in the article resonate with you? Are there other influences that you think are overlooked? Discuss with a friend.
- In his book *Evangelism for "Normal" People*, John Bowen associates evangelism strategies that are dehumanizing and inappropriate with "flasher" evangelism (borrowing language from a Margaret Atwood short story). What strategies for talking about faith do you similarly find inappropriate or unhelpful? What would make them more constructive?
- Reach out to a friend, ministry colleague, or church community who has constructive practices of sharing testimony. Have a conversation with them about this practice and why they do it.
- Consider experimenting with practices of sharing testimony or faith stories in your church community—whether in a small group, a Bible study, or in worship. Consult the opening sections of Lillian Daniel's book *Tell It Like It Is* to consider her experience with reviving such practices.

3
Embodying the Story

> But among us you will find uneducated persons, and artisans, and old women, who, if they are unable in words to prove the benefit of our doctrine, yet by their deeds exhibit the benefit arising from their persuasion of its truth: they do not rehearse speeches, but exhibit good works; when struck, they do not strike again; when robbed, they do not go to law; they give to those that ask of them, and love their neighbors as themselves.
>
> —ATHENAGORAS, *PLEA FOR THE CHRISTIANS*, CHAPTER 11[1]

AT THE CONGREGATION I served as a pastor, there was an ongoing relationship with a community in rural Honduras. The congregation partnered with the community to sponsor a lunch program for children who otherwise lacked access to food. As part of this, each year the congregation sent a group of travelers to see the program and nurture the ongoing partnership. While there, medically trained members of our group offered health clinics, since the community also lacked access to medical care. Sometimes our group assisted with other local projects in the community. But for the most part, our group's time in Honduras was not focused on building projects, but on building relationships.

---

1. Trans. B. P. Pratten. In *ANF* 2:134.

During my years at the church, I had the opportunity to join the traveling groups several times. On one occasion, we met another US church group in the airport during a layover. They too were going to Honduras for humanitarian reasons. But their approach was very different. Instead of partnering with and visiting the same community, they went to places where they had not been. In these places, they set up medical clinics (a bit like we did), but with an expectation attached. They required those who attended first to hear an hour-long presentation of the gospel, followed by a call to commitment. After that, they were seen by a medical doctor. After being seen and treated, they were encouraged to find and get involved in a local church community. This was the pattern of the US church group, who carried it out at a new and different location each day of their travel.

During our layover, I talked with one of the group's leaders. He was surprised at our group's strategy. "How will people hear the gospel if you don't clearly present it?" On that point, we differed. I think the community members in Honduras with whom we partnered *did* hear the gospel as part of our partnership, just less by our words than by our actions. We did not go just to give but also to receive. We did not go to inform them of the gospel, since 80 to 90 percent of them already identified as Christian anyway. We did not go to evangelize simply by our words but also by our presence and collaboration.

I do not wish to suggest the other church group's strategy is entirely wrong. Under scrutiny, both our approaches have shortcomings. But I do think they run the risk of overemphasizing a verbal expression of the gospel, thereby underappreciating its holistic impact (as well as the value of reciprocal partnerships in ministry). People in desperate need of medical care are not an audience well primed to hear a message until their health needs are first met. In this case, medical services in the name of Jesus may be a more effective sermon about Jesus than a scripted message.

To inform our thinking about the relative value of these two evangelical strategies, we may learn some things from the early church, whose growth in the early centuries is significant and instructive. Clearly, the early church was a community of good news people. But they shared this message of good news not simply by their words. They also shared it through their deeds. The story of Acts has much to offer as we consider the witness of church communities in their earliest stages.

Embodying the Story

An Embodied Witness: Acts 2:42-47 and 4:32-37

Christians of all stripes look to Acts to learn some things about how the early church lived as a community of believers. What most readers pay less attention to is how this community carried itself in relation to everyone around them.

In Acts, the early community of Jesus followers (i.e., the church) gets a significant boost of growth in the wake of Pentecost (2:1-41).

> 41 So those who welcomed his message were baptized, and that day about three thousand persons were added. 42 They devoted themselves to the apostles' teaching and fellowship, to the breaking of bread and the prayers. 43 Awe came upon everyone because many wonders and signs were being done through the apostles. 44 All who believed were together and had all things in common; 45 they would sell their possessions and goods and distribute the proceeds to all, as any had need. 46 Day by day, as they spent much time together in the temple, they broke bread at home and ate their food with glad and generous hearts, 47 praising God and having the goodwill of all the people. And day by day the Lord added to their number those who were being saved. (Acts 2:41-47)

Luke ballparks those who join the community at Pentecost at "about three thousand." Like similar tallies by other ancient history writers, the number is more impressionistic than a certified accounting. As James Dunn points out, "Numbers in ancient historians tended to be more impressionistic (or propagandistic) rather than to provide what we today would regard as an accurate accounting."[2] Still, clearly a large number becomes affiliated with the movement at this point. In response to the Pentecost experience, the community devotes itself to learning and instruction, gathering and sharing, and worship and prayer. Daily they gather for worship and community in the temple vicinity and in homes, in both public and private spaces. It was clearly a special time in the life of the early church, marked by "many wonders and signs" attesting to the movement's validity and by increasing affiliation as "day by day the Lord added to their number" (v. 47). Whatever

---

2. Dunn, *Acts*, 34. Keener notes: "On the whole, historians were not careless, but even the best of them often had only approximations" (*Acts*, 1:995-96). Elsewhere in Acts Luke's language reflects a tendency toward hyperbole for rhetorical impact, using "all" language in ways that arguably exaggerate (4:16; 19:10; see also 17:6). These instances suggest Luke's numerical count in Acts 2:41—as well as 4:4—is more a generalized approximation than an accounting by modern standards. For further discussion of Luke's accounting in comparison to ancient writings, see Keener, *Acts*, 1:993-99.

happened historically, these depictions mark authentic aspects of the earliest community's experience, character, and life together.

Another mark of this distinctive season in the early community's life is the radical generosity in which it engaged. Two chapters later, Acts offers a similar description of the early community, which complements and builds upon that in Acts 2, but with additional details about practices of generosity:

> 32 Now the whole group of those who believed were of one heart and soul, and no one claimed private ownership of any possessions, but everything they owned was held in common. 33 With great power the apostles gave their testimony to the resurrection of the Lord Jesus, and great grace was upon them all. 34 There was not a needy person among them, for as many as owned lands or houses sold them and brought the proceeds of what was sold. 35 They laid it at the apostles' feet, and it was distributed to each as any had need. 36 There was a Levite from Cyprus, Joseph, to whom the apostles gave the name Barnabas (which means "son of encouragement"). 37 He sold a field that belonged to him, then brought the money and laid it at the apostles' feet. (Acts 4:32–37)

No other New Testament passage depicts the sharing of early Christians so vividly. In fact, the portrayal is so radical that some readers in the United States find it foreign and unrealistic. For people who live today in a highly individualistic, capitalist, wealthy society, such communal sharing is undoubtedly difficult to imagine.

Foreign or shocking as it may be for modern Westerners, the portrayal would have appealed to virtues widely held across ancient cultures and societies in the Mediterranean. Ancient Israel held "there will be no needy person among you" (Deut 15:4) as a scriptural ideal, to which Acts alludes (4:34). Plato held that shared wealth was a practice of the ideal state.[3] A host of ancient Greek writers recite the adage "friends share everything in common," implying that true friendship involves sharing tangible resources.[4] Roman writers like Pliny associate similar sharing practices with authentic hospitality (*Ep.* 1.4.3). Greek philosophical communities like the

---

3. Plato, *Republic* 4.420C–422B; 5.462B–464A; *Laws* 3.679BC, 684CD; 5.744B–746C; 6.757A. Plato believed this ideal was practiced to some extent in ancient Athens (*Critias* 110CD). On the early church in Acts and Plato, see Dupertuis, "Summaries."

4. Plato, *Republic* 4.424A, 449C; Aristotle, *Nicomachean Ethics* 8.11, 1159b 31; 9.8, 1168b 8; Euripides, *Andromache* 376–77; Plutarch, *Moralia* 767E; Terence, *Brothers* 803–4; Philo, *Abraham* 235; Iamblichus, *Life of Pythagoras* 19.92; Dio Chrysostom, *Kingship (Orations)* 3.110.

Pythagoreans practiced communal sharing in which "all things were common and the same for all, and no one possessed anything privately."[5] The Jewish Essene communities practiced a sharing of money and community goods that extended to sharing with neighbors.[6] And although there is skepticism about the extent to which such communities practiced these ideals, outside observers attest that such practices existed—and they do so with great admiration.[7] Finally, many early Christian writings express strong convictions about the importance of sharing material goods with those in need—and these convictions do not diminish quickly in the ensuing centuries.[8]

Further, there is good reason to think the earliest community did not engage in a strict liquidation of all personal assets into communal ownership, but instead in regular, generous practices of selling and distributing to those in need. Despite Luke's claim in Acts 4:32 ("no one claimed private ownership . . . , but everything they owned was held in common"), similar language appears elsewhere in Greek and Jewish literature to mark practices of significant generosity, but without precluding ongoing ownership by individuals.[9] While radical and distinctive, the focus was most likely more upon there being "not a needy person among them" (4:34) than instantiating a specific economic model.

At the end of the day, the earliest community in Acts serves as a positive answer to the calls of Jesus in Luke's Gospel to forsake possessions and to give to the poor. More distinctively than in all three other Gospels, in Luke Jesus challenges his followers to relinquish possessions as part of the

---

5. Iamblichus, *Life of Pythagoras* 30.168; see also 35.257. The ideal was to be of "one body and one soul," calling "that which is mine and that which belongs to another by the same name" (30.167). The Epicureans also strove to embody similar practices. The quotation ("friends share everything in common") is attributed to Pythagoras, whose disciples strove to practice the ideal (Diogenes Laertius, *Lives of Eminent Philosophers* 8.1.10).

6. Josephus, *Antiquities* 18.1.5 §20; *Jewish War* 2.8.3 §122; Philo, *Hypothethica* 11.4-5; *Good Person* 75-86; Pliny, *Natural History* 5.17.13.

7. Aulus Gellius 1.9.12; Pliny, *Natural History* 5.15.73.

8. 2 Cor 8-9; 1 Tim 6:7-10, 17-19; Jas 2:1-7; Didache 4:5-8; Irenaeus, *Against Heresies* 4.13.3; Basil the Great, *Sermon to the Rich*; John Chrysostom, *Homilies on Romans* 7.

9. So Walton, "Primitive Communism in Acts?" See also Lindemann, "Beginnings." This tempered view of the early church's practices of generosity allows more readily for the understanding that such practices did not entirely vanish after the earliest stages of the church (see Acts 6:1-6; 9:36; 10:2; 11:27-30).

call to discipleship.[10] The early church in Acts, then, responds positively to these challenges, even if not perfectly (cf. 5:1–11). Not just at the start, but also throughout Acts, church communities engage in regular practices of relinquishment, generosity, and sharing with those in need (6:1–6; 9:36; 10:2; 11:27–30).

The portrayal of Acts 4:32–37 concludes with a specific example of generosity (Barnabas), which stands in contrast to an example of ungenerosity right afterward (Ananias and Sapphira, 5:1–11). Together, the two stories are not simply opposing reactions to the call to share—they are acts of opposing forces. Whereas Barnabas's generosity is a response to the Spirit's presence and power (cf. 4:31, 36–37), the deceit of Ananias and Sapphira is attributed to Satan (5:3). While the two donations may look similar, the cosmic powers at work help explain Ananias and Sapphira's deceit and condemnation, making the story less about a couple's misstep than about the tragic entry of evil into the Spirit's community. Together, the pairing of 4:36–37 and 5:1–11 creates a portrayal of contrasting paths: generosity vs. deceit, self-divesting vs. honor accumulating, and the work of the Spirit vs. that of Satan—with the latter resulting in pain and death. In the end, the pairing attests to the significance of sharing in community as an act prompted by the Holy Spirit.

In whatever ways the earliest community practiced generosity, Acts notes something significant about how they were received. Not only was the community "praising God," it was also "having the goodwill [*charis*] of all the people" (2:47a). Other translations word it differently: "they were all held in high esteem" (New English Bible), and "they were all accorded great respect" (New Jerusalem Bible), for example. This goodwill, high esteem, or great respect was bestowed not by community members, but by "all" the peoples around. A very similar depiction is reiterated in Acts 4: "and great grace [*charis*] was upon them all" (v. 33b). Although the bestower of this grace (esteem, favor) is less clear, Luke typically makes his references to God's grace explicit, which suggests this instance—like 2:47a—refers to a great respect or high esteem among neighboring people.[11]

This goodwill among neighbors is not arbitrary or groundless. Several connecting words suggest a direct correlation to how the community *acted* in relation to its neighbors. Right after 4:33b, a conjunction absent from the

---

10. See Luke 12:13–21, 33–34; 18:22–30. See also the section below "Bearing Witness and the Way of Jesus."

11. See, for example, Luke 1:30; 2:40, 52; Acts 7:46.

NRSVue text appears (*gar*), meaning "for."[12] Tiny as the word is, it clearly connects what precedes to the tangible acts of generosity that follow: "and great grace was upon them all. *For* there was not a needy person among them . . ." (4:33b–34a, emphasis mine). Another connecting word precedes 4:33b (*te*), typically translated "so" or "and so." This word connects the goodwill (grace) among neighboring people with the "great power" with which the apostles gave their testimony: "With great power the apostles gave their testimony to the resurrection of the Lord Jesus, *and so* great grace was upon them all" (v. 33, my translation and emphasis).[13] Throughout Acts, "great power" is language often associated with miraculous signs that inspire faith (8:13). In the depiction of 4:32–37, the only miraculous signs explicitly named are the acts of radical sharing by the community. This means the community's generosity itself has become a tangible sign that authenticates the message of Jesus and inspires faith among all.

In sum, the high regard that surrounding peoples had for the earliest community (Acts 2:47a; 4:33b) is not random but is inspired by the ways in which the community cared for those in need. The community bore witness "with great power" to the message of Jesus, not by the force of their words, but by the ways they embodied their message about Jesus in community and in their interactions with others.

The Embodied Witness of the Early Church

Most readers notice how much of Acts is dedicated to speeches—many of which are spoken by apostles like Peter and Paul.[14] As a result, readers often come away from Acts with the impression faithful witness is primarily a matter of words.

But the apostles and early believing communities did far more than speak words. They embodied the message of Jesus through acts of tending to the needs of those around them. They shared their resources with those in need, strove to address the needs of the sick, tended to the distribution

---

12. Since the word (*gar*) is a postpositive, technically it appears second in v. 34, but only due to grammatical propriety.

13. For this specific instance, BDAG defines *te* as a "marker of close relationship between sequential states or events, *and likewise, and so, so*" (993, italics original).

14. Aune estimates about 25 percent of the narrative is dedicated to speeches (*New Testament*, 125). Soards points out that 365 of the roughly thousand verses in Acts (36.5 percent) are given to both speeches and dialogue (*Speeches in Acts*, 1).

of food to widows, collaborated to send relief to famine-affected regions, attended to people in prison, and offered hospitality to traveling ministers of Jesus.[15] Throughout Acts, practices of generosity, almsgiving, and hospitality are a way of life for Jesus-followers. As church communities spread across the Mediterranean region, they became increasingly like a social network that collaborated to care for people both within and outside each community's boundaries.

The depiction of Acts was not merely an ideal. It reflects many historic practices that are attested by various sources as part of the way and ethos of early church communities. Early followers of Jesus cared for those in need of healing, attended to people in prison, took in widows and orphans, and prioritized hospitality toward guests. In many ways, they tended to people and groups who otherwise were overlooked. In the late second century, Tertullian observes:

> [Our gifts and offerings] are not taken and spent on feasts, and drinking-bouts, and eating-houses, but to support and bury poor people, to supply the needs of boys and girls who lack property and parents, and then for old slaves and mariners who have suffered shipwreck, and those who are in mines, on islands, or in prisons. [We do all this] out of loyalty to the cause of the school of God, and by this we become adherents (*alumni*) of our confession. But this work of such great love brings a branding upon us in the eyes of some. (Tertullian, *Apology* 39.6–7a, my translation)

Virtually all these activities came with a cost to early Jesus-followers—whether in money, time, work, or social capital. These acts of generosity and hospitality were neither convenient nor easy. But they played a critical role in the impression set by early church communities throughout the early centuries. Henry Chadwick suggests early Christian practices of generosity were "probably the most potent single cause of Christian success" in spreading geographically as it did.[16] They contributed to what Tertullian called a "branding" upon them in the eyes of others, which became part of their testimony—one that entailed more than words. This testimony was

---

15. Sharing with those in need: Acts 2:45; 4:34; 6:1–6; 11:28–30. Addressing the sick with healing: 3:1–10; 5:12–16; 9:32–43; 14:8–10; 20:9–10; 28:7–10. Tending to the needs of widows: 6:1–6; 9:36–42 (see also Jas 1:27; 1 Tim 5:3–16). Sending relief aid to regions affected by famine: Acts 11:28–30 (see also 24:17). Almsgiving: 9:36; 10:2; 24:17. Attending to those in prison: 12:12; 23:16 (see also Heb 13:3). Offering hospitality: Acts 16:11–15; 20:1–16; 21:1–16; 28:14–15.

16. Chadwick, *Early Church*, 55–56.

embodied by early believers' acts of generosity, hospitality, and conduct with neighbors and in larger society.

One's Way of Life as Testimony

The basic idea that practices speak as loudly as words was not invented by early Christians. Throughout the ancient Mediterranean world where they lived, this idea was widely known, especially among schools of philosophy.

Plato's *Apology*, which narrates Socrates's defense, is essentially an elaborate argument that the conduct of one's life—especially in the face of death—is the most honest and persuasive testimony to the value of one's creed.[17] This idea was influential among later Greek and Roman philosophical schools, which were movements dedicated to moral questions about ethical living. The Cynic philosopher Epictetus (early second century CE) argues that the philosopher's life and embodiment of his teaching serve as "witnesses to the truth of [their] contention."[18] He even held that philosophers served as "witnesses" to others about the purposes of Zeus.[19] Although from a later time period (late third century CE), the Neoplatonist philosopher Porphyry summarizes: "it is [one's] actions that naturally afford demonstrations of [her or] his opinions; and whoever holds a belief must live in accordance with it, in order that [s/]he may [her/]himself be a faithful witness to [her or] his disciples of [her or] his words."[20] For both philosophical schools and people in general throughout antiquity, the proof of a belief system was how its devotees lived.

---

17. "Strange, indeed, would be my conduct, O men of Athens, . . . if I disobeyed the [divine] oracle [to fulfill the philosopher's mission] because I was afraid of death: then I should be fancying to be wise when I was not wise" (Plato, *Apology* 28d–29a, trans. Jowett).

18. Epictetus, *Discourses* 3.22.88–90 (trans. Oldfather). So also: "What, then, is the thing lacking now? The man to make use of them, the man to bear witness to the arguments by his acts" (1.29.56–58).

19. "And of this Zeus wished me to get a demonstration in my own person . . . and to present me before all other men as a witness about the things which lie outside the sphere of the moral purpose" (3.24.110–14). So also: "Does God so neglect his own creatures, his servants, his witnesses, whom alone he uses as examples to the uninstructed, to prove that he both is, and governs the universe well, and does not neglect the affairs of men, and that no evil befalls a good man either in life or in death?" (3.26.28). For more on Epictetus's understanding of the philosopher's testimony or "witness," see Strathmann, "μάρτυς, μαρτυρέω, μαρτυρία, μαρτύριον," 480–81.

20. *Letter to Marcella* 8 (trans. Zimmern).

This is a major reason why Paul invites hearers of his letters to join in imitating him and his life.²¹ It was not because Paul had an inflated ego or because he thought his capacity to live out the gospel was superior. It was because throughout antiquity, among those familiar with philosophical ideas or who simply breathed the air of Greco-Roman culture, there was an assumption in widespread circulation: the true test of a creed's worth may be seen in how its followers and teachers live. And so, whether Paul invited imitation of his way of life or not, people would have judged his message and learned most about it from how he lived. The faith and message of Jesus, after all, is more than an abstract theory—it is a way of life. This is why Paul invited people: "Be imitators of me, as I am of Christ" (1 Cor 11:1).

Bearing Witness and the Way of Jesus

Paul's invitation taps into something important from early Christianity. For early church communities in Acts and throughout the early centuries, the call to bear witness to Jesus by a distinctive way of life was not simply a nice idea. It sprang from the call to embody the pattern and way of life seen first in Jesus.

On this point, Acts is especially clear. In ways that make for close parallels, the early church in Acts lives out and embodies the ministry of Jesus as seen in Luke's Gospel. Like Jesus does in Luke's Gospel, early apostles and church communities in Acts travel widely, preach and teach in synagogues and public places, heal and perform miracles, engage marginalized people, live an anti-accumulating lifestyle, encounter evil and opposition, see unexpected positive and negative responses, suffer under Jewish and Roman authorities, are imprisoned, and at times relinquish their lives.²² Through-

---

21. "Be imitators of me" (1 Cor 4:16), "as I am of Christ" (11:1); "join in imitating me, and observe those who live according to the example you have in us" (Phil 3:17; so also 4:9); "become as I am, for I also have become as you are" (Gal 4:12). Paul also praises the Thessalonian churches for having become imitators of Paul and his colleagues and of other churches (1 Thess 1:6; 2:14; so also 2 Cor 8–9). On Paul and tropes from the moral philosophers, see Malherbe, *Paul and the Thessalonians*, ch. 2.

22. The apostles and early believers in Acts heal and perform miracles in Jesus' name (3:6, 16; 4:10, 30; 16:18; cf. 19:13), encounter evil and opposition (13:4–12; also 5:1–11), experience unexpected negative and positive responses (9:23–25; 13:50; 14:5–6; 17:5–10, 32; 18:6; 19:23—20:1; 28:24–28), are imprisoned (4:3; 5:18; 8:3; 9:2; 12:3–5; 16:16–40; 22:22–29; see also 21:11–14), and sometimes suffer the same fate of death (7:54–60; 12:2; see also 9:23; 14:19; 20:22–25; 21:31–32). For parallels between the experiences of Jesus in Luke's Gospel and those of the apostles in Acts, see Mattill, "Jesus-Paul Parallels";

out hardships, both Jesus and early church people also experience signs of the Spirit's presence: being filled by the Spirit, anointed by the Spirit, or privy to an unexplainable, divine joy.[23] In both narratives and in parallel ways, Jesus and the church embody and proclaim a message of salvation embodied in Jesus the Messiah.[24]

Take the specific example of wealth and possessions. The early church did not invent practices of radical generosity. It was taught and embodied first by its Lord. More than in any other Gospel account, Luke's Jesus gives repeated, pointed, radical calls to relinquish possessions and a lifestyle of accumulation for the sake of following him:

- Blessed are you who are poor, for yours is the kingdom of God. . . . But woe to you who are rich, for you have received your consolation. (Luke 6:20, 24)
- None of you can become my disciple if you do not give up all your possessions. (14:33)
- You cannot serve God and mammon (wealth). (16:13)

These are a small sampling—all of which are unique to Luke's Gospel, with its pointed focus on the faithful use of resources.[25] In response to the teachings of Jesus, the church in Acts embodies practices of generosity and sharing. They do so not just for generosity's sake, but in response to the call of Jesus. In doing so, the church embodies the way of Jesus in its practices of community together.

O'Toole, "Parallels"; Talbert, *Literary Patterns*, 17–18, 22.

23. The apostles pray in the face of threats (4:23–31), sing in prison cells (16:25), behold heaven on the threshold of death (7:54–60), and rejoice in persecution (5:41). These experiences of joy and transcendence do not stem from the apostles themselves, but from the experiences and circumstances of walking the path of Jesus.

24. Luke Timothy Johnson summarizes: "Luke shows the church in Acts continuing the prophetic witness of Jesus in the Gospel: the church is filled with the spirit, speaks God's word, embodies that word in prayer, itinerancy, sharing possessions, and servant leadership, and enacts that word through a ministry of healing and embrace. All of this constitutes its witness at the most fundamental level" (*Prophetic Jesus*, 181). Van Unnik suggests "Acts is the confirmation (*bebaiōsis*) of what God did in Christ as told in the first book" ("Confirmation," 58, italics original). See also O'Toole, "Activity."

25. Other distinctive Lukan teachings and parables about wealth are John's words to soldiers and tax collectors (Luke 3:10–14), the parable of the rich fool (12:13–21), the parable of the shrewd manager (16:1–14), and the parable of Lazarus and the rich man (16:19–31; see also 4:18 and 19:1–10). Similar teachings in Luke's Gospel, which are shared by other Gospel writers, are 18:18–30 and 19:11–27.

According to Acts, embodied faithful witness takes shape by simply living out the way of Jesus, however imperfectly, for the world to see. In doing so, followers of Jesus make his presence known and visible. In walking the path and embodying his way, followers of Jesus live out the calling to be his witnesses in diverse ways, not just in word, but also in deed.

The Power of an Embodied Witness

Many people today associate evangelism and witness with a spoken message. While it may be part of the package, spoken words are only *part* of it. After all, a community (or individual) who says one thing in words and another in actions will not offer a persuasive message.

The best example of this is Jesus, who taught pointedly about the sharing of wealth, not just in word but also in deed. He challenged followers to a life of generosity not just by his teachings, but also by the way he lived: as an itinerant, essentially homeless teacher, who frequented poor rural areas, ate with outcasts, and challenged those in authority to relinquish resources to assist the needy. Radical as Jesus' teachings on generosity were, no one accused him of hypocrisy. He taught a way of life by both his words as well as his actions.

Faithful witness, after all, is an act of testifying to the truth. In matters of personal experience, that involves testifying about historic events. In these cases, truthfulness is associated with historical accuracy. But in matters of God and faith, attesting to truth is a bit different. Things related to God and faith do not have clear-cut, scientific criteria for gauging truthfulness. Instead, the truthfulness of testimony about God is most often measured by the integrity of the witness. That is, the truthfulness of a testimony depends greatly on how authentically that message is integrated and embodied by the witness's life.

In 2021 Barna conducted a poll among Generation Z people (born 1997—early 2010s), asking non-Christian respondents: "If a Christian wanted to tell you about their faith, how appealing would the following approach be?" Among ten options, ranging from shared testimony to event invitations, the overwhelming favorite—the *only* option deemed "appealing" or "very appealing" by most respondents—was "Seeing how the person behaves, allowing their actions to speak rather than using words to explain their faith to me."[26] Clearly younger people today place greater value upon

---

26. Barna, "What Makes an Engaging Witness." The option cited received "very

an embodied (vs. spoken) witness than past generations have. This is worth paying careful attention to.

At an urban church congregation where I interned, there was a man in the neighborhood who often stopped by, "Doug." He was middle-aged, Native American, Christian by upbringing, and very personable. A seasonal worker and homeless by some definitions, he relied off and on upon social service agencies and the kindness of church communities. Most of the time, Doug stopped by our church just to talk. Somehow, he felt welcome and safe with us. He didn't feel that way about every church in the neighborhood—not even most. "They all say they're welcoming, but they don't really mean it." Some had safety concerns about him. Others wanted him to become their kind of Christian before helping him. Many simply didn't take the time to listen. And Doug was profoundly perceptive about the welcome he received at each place. That told him more than anything else what the community's faith was like.

An anonymous expression states: "You may be the only Bible some people ever read." Its point is this: our lives may be the only exposure some have to the message of Jesus. Our embodied witness may be the only preaching some people hear. People take notice how faith communities, their leaders, and their people live. And it makes an impression. More to the point, it offers an unspoken testimony.

First Steps: Embodying the Story

Faithful embodied witness is not rocket science. It starts with simply living out Jesus' call to "love your neighbor as yourself" in tangible and intentional ways. This kind of love has no strings attached. This kind of love values people just as they are, not as we think they should be. This kind of love acts with kindness toward someone, not for the sake of what the giver may receive, but to embody kindness to someone made in the image of God. This kind of love acts toward others in the same way we believe God in Jesus Christ first acted toward us. As 1 John words it, "we love because God first loved us" (4:19).

Embodying the good news of Jesus is less about specific acts than it is a way of life—a way in which we act, live, and share with love toward other people. As such, it may be measured less by specific steps than by areas of

---

appealing" responses from 23 percent of respondents and "appealing" from 32 percent of respondents (= 55 percent). No other response received more than 12 percent very appealing or more than 37 percent combined of appealing and very appealing.

our lives that are changed, influenced, or different. As individuals, we might start with questions that take stock of how the following areas of our lives bear witness to the faith of Jesus:

- Our finances and generosity (sharing)
- Our participation in our larger community
- Our treatment of our neighbors
- Our beliefs about people with whom we disagree
- Our preoccupation with consumption and accumulation (vs. simplicity)
- Our behavior on social media
- Our behavior in traffic
- Our treatment of customer service employees
- Our random acts of kindness
- Our advocacy for those without voice
- Our investment in young people

These examples are primarily on an individual or household level. When it comes to how we act as communities, especially communities of faith, we can consider not only the areas above, but also bigger changes and possibilities:

- Our intentionality about welcoming newcomers
- Our commitment to caring for one another
- Our investment in raising up leaders
- Our relationships with neighbors
- Our work addressing poverty and related challenges in our local community
- Our support of agencies in our local community doing the most good for people in need
- Our care for people, regardless of whether they join our church
- Our intentionality about ecumenical and interreligious partnerships
- Our investment in global partnerships and ministry
- Our faithful use of offerings and resources
- Our fostering of a culture of grace and acceptance

These are all possible areas for faithful witness in Jesus' name—areas where our message may speak without requiring words. They are less things for us to "go out and do" (and so be done with) than areas of our lives through which the grace and love of God may shine. Whether straightforward or challenging, these areas of our lives have great potential for seeing tangible differences made in Jesus' name.

Yang Tut did not become a Christian church leader by chance. Growing up in his native country of Sudan, he went through a great deal of chaos and traumatic events. During those years, he received international aid in different ways and at different times. On one occasion, he remembers stacked boxes of aid supplies with the name "Lutheran" written on the side. Wherever the aid came from, he knew they came from Lutherans. Years later, he immigrated to the United States—and he remembered that experience. So he joined a Lutheran church. He is now an ordained pastor in the Lutheran church, with a focus upon serving South Sudanese immigrants.[27]

Conclusion

Bearing witness to our faith is not just a matter of words. It involves embodying a message of grace and a way of life made known to us in Jesus Christ. It is embodied by individuals and communities. And it is a witness that others most readily observe.

I hope you experience this chapter as an invitation and opportunity to reflect on the significance of our lives as walking testimonies. Especially for those who do not excel at talking about faith, this is a word of good news: we are called to bear witness to the message of Jesus, whether or not it is verbally expressed. In words often attributed to Saint Francis of Assisi: Preach the gospel at all times, and if necessary use words.[28]

A friend of mine ("Jim") lived in Grand Forks, North Dakota, when a major flood happened. It was a national disaster that put an overwhelming majority of homes and residences underwater. In response, aid organizations and church groups from across the country showed up to help. Early

---

27. Story used with permission.

28. No surviving writing by or about Saint Francis has this quote, but a statement from his *Rule of 1221* has something similar: "No brother may preach contrary to the forms and institutions of the holy church.... All the brothers, however, should preach by their actions" (17, trans. Schwartz and Lachance, in Flood and Matura, *Birth of a Movement*, 63–85).

in the process, Jim received a knock at his door. Two fellows stood outside. "We're from Arkansas. We're part of a church group and we're here with _____ relief agency to help. What can we do?" Soon after, they were mucking out his basement—a messy and unenjoyable task for anyone. As they worked, Jim reflected: "If this doesn't change my heart, I don't know what will." It became a significant moment for his sense of how faith compels us to help others. He later served as council president of the church where I served.

Sometimes the gospel needs hands and feet, more than words, to be authentically expressed.

Questions for Discussion

1. Who in your life has embodied the message of Jesus for you, not necessarily in words? What do you learn from their witness?

2. This chapter suggests the early church community lived in a way that was experienced positively by its neighbors. How do church communities continue that pattern today?

3. If someone were to ask random people in your larger community about your church, what do you think people would say? What do you hope people would say?

4. Luke Timothy Johnson points out: throughout history the church has often been a "sign of wealth rather than of poverty and has aligned itself with the rich and powerful on earth more than the weak and lowly." Meanwhile, "we remember that when Jesus announced that the poor were blessed because theirs was the kingdom of God, he did so not as a wealthy benefactor but as one who shared the state of the poor."[29] How might the church embody the way of Jesus more faithfully in its use of resources?

5. Ponder the following quote from Martin Luther about the call to serve the neighbor:

> The prince should think: Christ has served me and made everything to follow him; therefore, I should also serve my neighbor[s], protect [them] and everything that belongs to [them]. That is why

---

29. L. T. Johnson, *Prophetic Jesus*, 125 and 126.

God has given me this office, and I have it that I might serve him. That would be a good prince and ruler. When a prince sees his neighbor oppressed, he should think: That concerns me! I must protect and shield my neighbor. . . . The same is true for shoemaker, tailor, scribe, or reader. If [one] is a Christian tailor, [one] will say: I make these clothes because God has bidden me do so, so that I can earn a living, so that I can help and serve my neighbor. When a Christian does not serve the other, God is not present; that is not Christian living."[30]

How does this make you think about serving others at your workplace, in your station in life, or as a daily vocation?

Resources for Further Exploration

- Acts 2:41–47 and 4:32–37 as portrayals of the generosity of the early church. Other passages for further consideration are as follows:

    a. Sharing with those in need: Acts 2:45; 4:34; 6:1–6; 11:28–30.

    b. Addressing the sick with healing: Acts 3:1–10; 5:12–16; 9:32–43; 14:8–10; 20:9–10; 28:7–10.

    c. Tending to the needs of widows: Acts 6:1–6; 9:36–42 (see also Jas 1:27; 1 Tim 5:3–16).

    d. Sending relief aid to regions affected by famine: Acts 11:28–30 (see also 24:17).

    e. Almsgiving: Acts 9:36; 10:2; 24:17.

    f. Attending to those in prison: Acts 12:12; 23:16 (see also Heb 13:3).

    g. Offering hospitality: Acts 16:11–15; 20:1–16; 21:1–16; 28:14–15.

- Bass, Diana Butler, and J. Stewart-Sicking, editors. *From Nomads to Pilgrims: Stories from Practicing Congregations.* Washington, DC: Rowman & Littlefield, 2005.

---

30. Sermon in the Castle Church at Weimar (October 25, 1522), trans. Gaiser ("What Luther *Didn't* Say," 361), *Luthers Werke* 10/3:382.

- Gutenson, Charles E. "The Early Fathers on Wealth and Poverty," chapter 5 of *The Right Church: Live Like the First Christians*, 81–95. Nashville: Abingdon, 2012.
- Johnson, Luke Timothy. *Prophetic Jesus, Prophetic Church: The Challenge of Luke-Acts to Contemporary Christians*. Grand Rapids: Eerdmans, 2011. Chapters 6–7 (pp. 96–165).
- Walton, Steve. "Primitive Communism in Acts? Does Acts Present the Community of Goods (2:44–45; 4:32–35) as Mistaken?" In *Reading Acts Theologically*, 63–73. The Library of New Testament Series 661. London: T. & T. Clark, 2022.

Action Steps for Further Consideration

- Identify a faith community with a highly constructive, embodied witness in its surrounding community. Visit, explore, and learn more from this community about why and how they do what they do.
- Consider polling or talking to the people who live nearby your church community. What impressions do they have—positive or negative—of your church community?
- Consider what your church is known for in the community. What would you like it to be known for? (Example: "This is the church that does _____.") Consider action steps that might advance that purpose.
- Learn more about poverty and hunger in your local community. If appropriate, start a hunger ministry at your church that assists with local needs in effective and sustainable ways.
- Look into creative ways you and your church community can be more active with local programs to address homelessness, domestic abuse, immigration challenges, and injustices related to racism and sexism.

4

Making the Story Public

> It is in the public square that we might already find the new things of God taking place. And it is the church that needs to seek after the Lord, who is found in spaces the church sometimes does not imagine itself to be.
>
> —Elizabeth Conde-Frazier[1]

I ONCE PARTICIPATED IN a table conversation at a gathering of pastors. One pastor shared about a church near his own. The church regularly set up a booth at a public space to talk with passers-by about the gospel. This pastor had concerns about their approach, which was rather directive and confrontational. Others at the table shared the concern.

In response, another pastor asked: "How might we do something comparable but better?" She asked an honest question. Silence followed. People appreciated the question. No one had constructive answers.

This kind of quandary happens often among people interested in bringing the gospel into public spaces, but without being insensitive or off-putting. It's easy to point fingers at negative examples. It's more difficult to give constructive alternatives.

Bearing witness in public settings today is complicated, challenging, and fruitful when done well. It may even require a measure of boldness—a kind that comes from outside ourselves. This boldness is something that

1. Conde-Frazier, *Atando Cabos*, 105.

appears in the early chapters of Acts, as an experience and characteristic of the early church's witness.

Bold Witness: Acts 3–4

Soon after a community of believers is formed (Acts 2), a public incident takes place involving Peter and John. They don't go out looking for it. It happens due to their faithful response to an encounter.

Peter and John go to the temple area one afternoon at 3:00, a designated hour for prayer (3:1).[2] At the gate entrance, they find a man crippled from birth who frequently asked for alms. In response to him, Peter states: "I have no silver or gold, but what I have I give you; in the name of Jesus Christ of Nazareth, stand up and walk" (3:6). To the surprise of all, as Peter helps the man up, he is made well. He accompanies Peter and John into the temple, "walking and leaping and praising God" (v. 8). As people gather around to see, Peter addresses the crowd with words that attribute the miracle to faith in Jesus, whom God raised from the dead (3:11–16). This God sent Jesus first to the descendants of Abraham, "to bless you by turning each of you from your wicked ways" (v. 26).

---

2. Both the Mishnah and Josephus identify 3:00 p.m. with the afternoon (originally evening) sacrifice (*Pesahim* 5:1; Josephus, *Antiquities* 14.4.3 §65), which was a time when people near and far offered incense and prayer (Dan 9:21; Judith 9:1). Pious Jews typically said morning and evening prayers individually, and communal gatherings for prayer happened twice or three times a day in the temple area. How established and regular the patterns of prayer were for the temple and for synagogues is debated. Some see in Acts evidence for three hours of prayer: 9:00 a.m. (Acts 2:15), noon (10:9), and 3:00 p.m. (3:1; 10:3; see also Luke 1:10). See Falk, "Jewish Prayer."

St. Peter Healing (early 17th century), by Simone Cantarini (photo by Fondazione Carifano), public domain, courtesy of Wikimedia Commons

Not everyone in Jerusalem is pleased. A group of temple authorities arrests Peter and John, bringing them the next day before a gathering of rulers, elders, and scribes. On trial, the apostles are asked: "By what power or by what name did you do this?" (4:7) The scene continues as follows:

> 8 Then Peter, filled with the Holy Spirit, said to them, "Rulers of the people and elders, 9 if we are being questioned today because of a good deed done to someone who was sick and are being asked how this man has been healed, 10 let it be known to all of you, and to all the people of Israel, that this man is standing before you in good health by the name of Jesus Christ of Nazareth, whom

you crucified, whom God raised from the dead. 11 This Jesus is 'the stone that was rejected by you, the builders; it has become the cornerstone.' 12 There is salvation in no one else, for there is no other name under heaven given among mortals by which we must be saved." (Acts 4:8–12)

Even more instructive is the religious leaders' reaction that follows:

Now when they saw the boldness of Peter and John and realized that they were uneducated and ordinary men, they were amazed and recognized them as companions of Jesus. When they saw the man who had been cured standing beside them, they had nothing to say in opposition. (Acts 4:13–14)

Several pieces in this passage call for further discussion.

First, the religious leaders do not marvel at the persuasiveness of Peter and John's words as much as their "boldness" or "fearlessness" (*parrēsia*). This has nothing to do with mere volume. In popular Greek and Roman culture, philosophers and moralists praised this as frank, open, and fearless speech more committed to the truth than popular opinion. In contrast to flattery, fearless speech often proved insulting, making it prone to result in hostility and social repercussions.[3] Many ancient writers comment on the appropriateness of truthful, fearless speech before rulers and authorities, which was unconventional, potentially admirable, and very risky.[4] Regardless of its reception and outcome, fearless speech was widely associated with courage, freedom, and fidelity to the truth.[5]

In Acts this boldness refers to a fearless witness that is inspired by the presence and power of the Holy Spirit. It begins at Pentecost (2:29), continues with Peter and others in the early church community (4:13, 29, 31), and later appears characteristically with Paul throughout his ministry in new territories (9:27–28).[6] On each occasion, the Spirit enables people to proclaim the

---

3. See, for example, Philostratus, *Heroicus* 33.8–9; Lucian, *Philosophies for Sale* 8, 10.

4. Agrippa's former general, for example, asserted himself by speaking truthfully to Agrippa about his behavior, with the result that he remained imprisoned (Josephus, *Antiquities* 19.7.1 §§317–25). See also Dio Chrysostom, *Orations* 3.2–3, 13; 32.27–28; Iamblichus, *Life of Pythagoras* 32.215, 220; Philostratus, *Life of Apollonius* 8.4.

5. See, for example, Epictetus, *Diatribe* 1 preface; Lucian, *Nigrinus* 15; *Demonax* 3; Musonius Rufus, "That Exile Is not an Evil," 9.4–7, 12–13. For more on this, see Keener, *Acts*, 2:1152–54. On Paul's embodiment of frank speech in his letters, see Sampley, "Paul's Frank Speech."

6. Based upon occurrences of both the noun *parrēsia* and the verb *parrēsiazomai* ("proclaim boldly"). The Spirit explicitly "fills" Peter and the early community (4:8, 29,

message of Jesus in both private and public spaces, especially public ones. Quite often, this fearless speech takes shape before ruling authorities (4:13, 29; 26:26; 28:31). In cases like these, the Spirit's empowerment fulfills an earlier promise of Jesus: "When they bring you before the synagogues, the rulers, and the authorities, do not worry about how or what you will answer or what you are to say, for the Holy Spirit will teach you at that very hour what you ought to say" (Luke 12:11–12). In sum, this boldness or fearlessness of speech in Acts is a gift of the Spirit that enables faithful witness about Jesus in otherwise threatening and difficult environments.

Second, in the eyes of their audience, Peter and John are not conventionally credentialed. The religious authorities identify the two as "uneducated and ordinary men" (Acts 4:13). While "uneducated" (*agrammatoi*) normally refers to a lack of formal education, here it stands specifically in contrast to the status of trained religious professionals. Although Peter and John learned from Jesus, he is elsewhere deemed "uneducated" since he did not learn from a recognized teacher or school (John 7:15). Although the word "ordinary" (*idiōtēs*) is not as condescending as its closest English cognate ("idiot"), it's still not a compliment. It refers to someone who is a novice, untrained, unacquainted, or ignorant.[7] Together, "uneducated" and "ordinary" characterize Peter and John as uncredentialed rookies in religious matters. This is partially why the authorities are so amazed.

In the same observation, the two are recognized as "companions of Jesus"—or more literally, "they were with Jesus" (Acts 4:13). On an earlier occasion, Peter was ashamed of being associated with Jesus (Luke 22:56, 58). Now Peter embraces the identity publicly. People in antiquity often judged teachers by how their students turned out.[8] It was no different here. And whatever it is about Peter's and John's presence, words, disposition, and actions, they are immediately identified as people who have spent time

---

31) and anoints Paul (9:17–18). Later instances of such boldness by apostles continue this trajectory, since they appear in association with proclaiming the message of Jesus (13:46; 14:3; 18:26; 19:8; 26:26; 28:31)—which is portrayed throughout Luke-Acts as a Spirit-inspired endeavor (Luke 12:11–12; Acts 2:1–21). Van Unnik, "Christian's Freedom," 477–82; Hull, *Holy Spirit*, 143–45. Van Unnik argues it "is always mentioned in connection with preaching in the synagogues and to the Jews" in Acts (478), but that is not always the case (see Acts 4:29, 31; 26:26; 28:31).

7. Paul and Josephus both use the word to refer to people without rhetorical skill (2 Cor 11:6; *Antiquities* 2.12.2 §271) and outsiders in general (2 Cor 14:23–24).

8. See Mark 2:18, 24. See also Aeschines, *Timarchus* 171–73; Philostratus, *Lives of the Sophists* 2.8.579; 2.10.588; *Edduyot* 3:4; *Avot of Rabbi Nathan* 27A; Diogenes, *Epistle* 9 (to Crates). On Diogenes, see Malherbe, *Cynic Epistles*.

with and learned from Jesus. Luke's wording suggests that the leaders' recognition of this stems not from historic recollection, but from how Peter and John fearlessly bear witness to their message about Jesus, even under authoritative scrutiny. Their witness is further supported by the tangible evidence of a miraculous healing (i.e., the healed man), the very kind of thing Jesus once did. This makes the apostles' claims of Jesus' power difficult to refute. After all, the man was born crippled, widely known as such, and aged by ancient standards (Acts 3:2, 10; 4:22).

Third, this Spirit-inspired boldness flies in the face of what was expected. In a cultural world heavily dictated by public honor and shame, people of less authority normally cowered apologetically to social superiors, at the very least in deference to their social status.[9] This is why the apostles' defiance infuriates the Jerusalem authorities: it shames the authorities by disrespecting their social status. In a society that values social honor above all things, this was a direct affront. After all, the gathering of rulers, elders, priests, and scribes in Acts 4 constitutes the ruling council of Jerusalem's leaders—commonly known as the Sanhedrin (4:15; cf. Luke 22:66). Although predominately made up of religious leaders, it was effectively the city's municipal and governing body, who placed religious concerns at the forefront of civic concerns. While under Roman rule, this council had authority for legislative, executive, and judicial functions related to the welfare of the city and its region.[10] As long as Roman prefects and governors allowed, the Sanhedrin oversaw most of the city's business. More to the point, this is the same legislative body that set in motion the trial proceedings that resulted in Jesus' execution (Luke 22:47—23:25). If there were any doubts about the power of the Sanhedrin, that event quelled them.

But Peter and John's fearless profession reflects allegiance to a higher authority. Later in the scene, the authorities order the apostles to refrain from proclaiming and teaching in Jesus' name. Peter and John respond: "Whether it is right in God's sight to heed you more than God, you be the judge. For we cannot keep from speaking about the things we have seen and heard" (Acts 4:19-20). Their boldness stands in stark contrast to the Sanhedrin's silence—and desire for silence. In the very next chapter, Peter and the apostles voice the same idea more pointedly when called to account for disobeying the authorities again: "We must obey God rather than any

---

9. Toner, *Popular Culture*, 140.

10. Saldarini, "Sanhedrin," 975–80. The term "Sanhedrin" (*sanedrion*) was used for other city councils in Achaia, though the word *boulē* ("senate") was more common. See Josephus, *Life* 12 §64; 13 §69; 34 §169; 58 §300; 61 §313; 68 §381.

human authority" (5:29).[11] This is why the apostles dare to defy Jerusalem's governing body so boldly: they answer ultimately to a higher authority, God.

However unintentionally, Peter and John's public acts land them in hot water. But in response, the Holy Spirit empowers them to act and speak fearlessly as witnesses of Jesus called to carry on his work, despite the objections of local authorities.

Being the Church in Public

In the United States, many people associate religious faith with something that is private and personal. One reason is the principle of separation between church and state. The principle stems from the First Amendment of the US Constitution, which prohibits governing authorities from establishing or endorsing a specific religion and from prohibiting its free exercise. While this bars authorities (at least in theory) from governing by religious principles that do not apply to all, it also puts a wedge between religious creeds and civic governance, as if religious faith should not inform, influence, and engage the wider public with good. As a result, practicing religious faith in public arenas may not come naturally.

The early church took shape in a world that neither knew a church/state separation nor thought about faith through a public/private lens. Even though it started in the context of an empire sometimes hostile to its existence, the church saw professing the faith of Jesus as something that was both private and public, both individual and communal, and both theological and sociopolitical. In their world, the distinctions often drawn in American society were foreign.

An example of this in Acts is how early believers met not only in homes but also in public spaces. In Jerusalem, early believers gathered in the temple area (2:46; 5:12, 42). In Philippi, they started at a riverside place of prayer (16:13, 16). In Ephesus, Paul spent two years gathering with people in a public lecture hall (19:9–10).[12] In addition, the apostles preach and

---

11. This sentiment has precedents in both Jewish literature (Dan 3:17–18; 6:22; 2 Macc 7:2; 4 Macc 5:16–38; Josephus, *Antiquities* 17.6.3 §§158–59) and Greek literature (Plato, *Apology* 29D: "Men of Athens, I respect and love you, but I shall obey the god rather than you").

12. The *scholē* or Tyrannus in Ephesus was likely a building used as a lecture hall or schoolroom for philosophical instruction, or possibly a guildhall for skilled artisans. Tyrannus was most likely either the consistent orator during regular hours (if a schoolroom for philosophical instruction) or the landlord (if a guildhall).

teach in a wide variety of public spaces: the temple vicinity, synagogues, city gates, riversides, harbor areas, marketplaces, and lecture halls—all across the Mediterranean world.[13] In fact, at key points early on, Acts emphasizes that Jesus-followers gathered and carried on together in *both* public spaces *and* in homes:

> Day by day, as they spent much time together in the temple, they broke bread at home. (2:46)

> And every day in the temple and at home, they did not cease to teach and proclaim Jesus as the Messiah. (5:42)

> I did not shrink from doing anything helpful, proclaiming the message to you and teaching you, publicly and from house to house. (20:20)

These aspects make for a distinctive emphasis in the portrayal of the church: it's not a private club. It's a global movement that infiltrates both domestic and public arenas. This church is not restricted to designated buildings. It's a way of being, patterned after the itinerant way of Jesus, moving and engaging throughout the world.

Beyond Acts, other sources also attest to how the early church gathered and acted in public spaces. In later centuries early Christians used waterside areas for baptisms and burial sites for gathering. Some suggest they may also have used urban buildings, gardens, retail shops, industrial warehouses, and public leisure spaces like bathhouses and rented dining rooms.[14] All this shows that at its outset the church inhabited and made use of public spaces regularly and often. In the absence of buildings exclusively dedicated to church gathering, the church moved in transient ways, taking up space in public arenas on a regular basis.

Pastor Jodi Houge started and served a church that has migrated and inhabited many different spaces. Since 2008, Humble Walk Church has gathered in different seasons for regular worship in a coffee shop, a storefront space, a public park, a long-term care facility, and an art house. It has also hosted monthly beer and hymns sing-alongs at a local Irish pub. One

---

13. The temple vicinity: Acts 3:1—4:3; 22:1–21; synagogues: 9:20; 13:5, 14–43; 17:1–3, 10, 17; 18:4, 19; 19:8; city gates: 14:13–18; riversides: 16:13; harbors: 20:18–38; marketplaces: 17:17; trial spaces: 17:22–31; lecture halls: 19:9–10. The apostles also proclaim in spaces designated for trial hearings: 4:5–21; 5:27–32; 6:12—7:53; 17:22–31; 22:30—23:10; 24:10–20; 25:6–12; 26:1–29.

14. See Adams, *Earliest Christian Meeting Places*.

year, the church held an Ash Wednesday beer and hymns event in the pub's back room. They did so not to evangelize the pub or to show off piety, but as gracious recipients of the pub's hospitality. As the pastor was marking ash crosses on people's foreheads, she got a request from tables in the main room to bring ashes to them. As she did so, people in the pub opened up, sharing some of their stories with the pastor, even though they had just met. Some waitstaff asked for ashes as well. And suddenly the boundary between the sacred space of the back room and the public space of the pub disappeared. It was a holy moment that emerged from a trusting partnership between a local establishment and a church intentional about being good guests and neighbors.[15]

Faithful witness in public spaces isn't just about doing churchy things elsewhere. It's about constructive witness to the message of Jesus in public spaces, which can happen in a host of different ways. In the community where I served as a pastor, there is a significant Somali population who own and operate several businesses. One of these is a restaurant started by female refugees. It gained the status of being an unofficial hub for the immigrant community in town. About ten years ago, someone vandalized the restaurant with a spray-painted Nazi symbol and the words "Go home." Two days later, someone threw a homemade firebomb through the restaurant window, causing over a quarter million dollars in damage to the restaurant and neighboring businesses. The damage was so severe that the restaurant would never recover its former status. In the wake of these events, Somalis in the community were heartbroken and scared.

A day later, around a hundred people from different faith traditions (mostly Christian) showed up outside the restaurant for a candlelight vigil, to show the owners they do not stand alone. They bore witness to their faith by standing publicly with a vulnerable people. It inspired the Somalis—and the entire community. In the days to come, several fundraisers and donations of support came from the larger community. These acts built bridges between the largely Muslim Somali community and several Christian church communities—bridges that were not in place before. In response, owners of the restaurant issued a public letter expressing their gratitude: "We are deeply grateful to be part of this community. We have hope in this country because of you residents. Thank you for your generosity."[16] As this example shows, bearing witness to the gospel may not require traditional

---

15. Story used with permission.
16. MPR News, "Minnesota Man"; Global Friends Coalition, "Response," 7.

forms of evangelism. It may involve simply showing up to stand with a neighbor in need.

Bearing Witness as Attesting to the Truth

Faithful witness does not only mean speaking an explicit message about Jesus. It can also involve attesting to what is true and just, in ways that reflect and resonate with the truth of the gospel. The message of Jesus, after all, is one of life and liberation for all. When obstacles keep people from experiencing that life and liberation, followers of Jesus are called to testify to that truth.

The language of bearing witness has many shades of meaning today. One of these is attesting to injustices, especially those experienced by marginalized people. Many African Americans, for example, have found the language appropriate for attesting to experiences of racism, discrimination, and injustice.[17] Within this framework, Thomas Hoyt Jr. describes practices of testimony as they have taken shape historically in the African American church:

> The practice of testimony is one that people sorely need, particularly in a society where many voices sound yet where public speech that is honest and empowering is rare. . . . Yet people without economic and political power often find that their voices are not heard at all. In this context, we need to consider what it means to testify. The Black Church's practice of testimony offers insights on matters that concern everyone who seeks a life that is truthful.[18]

Hoyt describes faithful witness or testimony as "people speak[ing] truthfully about what they have experienced and seen."[19] Especially for people who lack economic and sociopolitical power, truth-telling about injustice is a part of bearing witness to the gospel. While true in particular ways for African Americans, this nuance of bearing witness (as truth-telling) is also true for all followers of Jesus.

In certain respects, the activities of Peter and John in Acts 3–4 are forms of truth-telling in response to injustices. What sets events in motion, first off, is an injustice or need: a man crippled from birth who lives in

---

17. On this, see Richardson, *Bearing Witness While Black*.
18. Hoyt, "Testimony," 92.
19. Hoyt, "Testimony," 92.

poverty as a result. In response, they offer healing (3:1–8). When crowds and authorities marvel, Peter and John clarify who is to be credited (3:11–16; 4:5–12). When the Sanhedrin unjustly forbids them from speaking about Jesus, they protest and refuse (4:13–22). Although Peter and John seize opportunity to speak publicly about Jesus, the precipitating events all stem from injustices that compel the apostles to respond truthfully and faithfully, getting them into trouble with the authorities.

Bearing witness as truth-telling is risky, for several reasons. First, not everyone welcomes the truth. In Acts 4–5, the authorities are concerned with how the apostles' testimony highlights the authorities' role in Jesus' death (5:28). There is a zero-sum game of social honor in play here between Jesus and the authorities: to honor Jesus is to dishonor the authorities who had a hand in his death. To speak in Jerusalem about Jesus' death and exaltation so soon after the events is bound to provoke conflict.[20] Whatever truths are told, they will be inconvenient—if not defaming—for some, inviting negative response.

Second, bearing witness to truth related to the gospel is a divine claim. It lays claim to things about God, how God sees the world, and what God wants for people. This is an authoritative claim—and a provocative one. Many people do not appreciate someone making a claim about God that challenges or judges their convictions, beliefs, or habits. For this reason, in Acts some early witnesses become martyrs, as their testimony is deemed blasphemy by religious authorities.[21] Bearing witness to the truth of the gospel, after all, involves a calling to heed divine truth instead of alternative "truths," even when that creates a clash of claims. In Peter's words: "We must obey God rather than any human authority" (Acts 5:29).

In early December of 1955, a forty-two-year-old woman named Rosa Parks was arrested for refusing to give up her bus seat to a white person in Montgomery, Alabama. The incident was not an isolated one: it culminated years of ongoing discrimination in the community. And it was church leaders and communities that led the way in responding. Although

---

20. Many public proclamations to Jewish audiences in Acts place intentional focus upon the culpability of Jewish leaders and people. On this, see Tyson, "Problem of Jewish Rejection."

21. Stephen is the classic example (6:8—8:1), whose experience parallels Jesus' in Luke's Gospel (22:66—23:25). Although not charged of blasphemy per se, Paul is similarly charged with forms of apostasy (21:27–29; 24:5–8), leading to his eventual execution according to tradition (1 Clem. 5:7; cf. Acts 28:30–31). The Greek word for "witness" is *martyr*.

countless African American leaders, their allies, and around forty thousand others eventually joined the Montgomery Bus Boycott of 1955–56, the most significant organizers were church leaders like Martin Luther King Jr., Ralph D. Abernathy, L. Roy Bennett, Robert Graetz, and others. And it was churches like Dexter Avenue Baptist Church, Mt. Zion AME Zion Church, Holt Street Baptist Church, and others who hosted the critical organizational meetings that catalyzed the movement.[22] They did so not because it was convenient or advantageous, but because the truth of the gospel of Jesus compelled them. As the elected leader of the boycott, Martin Luther King Jr. stated in his rallying speech on December 5, 1955, at Holt Street Baptist Church:

> And we are not wrong, we are not wrong in what we are doing. If we are wrong, the Supreme Court of this nation is wrong. If we are wrong, the Constitution of the United States is wrong. If we are wrong, God Almighty is wrong. If we are wrong, Jesus of Nazareth was merely a utopian dreamer that never came down to earth. If we are wrong, justice is a lie. Love has no meaning. And we are determined here in Montgomery to work and fight until justice runs down like water, and righteousness like a mighty stream. . . . May I say to you my friends, as I come to a close, . . . whatever we do, we must keep God in the forefront. Let us be Christian in all of our actions. But I want to tell you this evening that it is not enough for us to talk about love, love is one of the pivotal points of the Christian face, faith. There is another side called justice. And justice is really love in calculation. Justice is love correcting that which revolts against love. . . . I've never been on a bus in Montgomery. But I would be less than a Christian if I stood back and said, because I don't ride the bus, I don't have to ride a bus, that it doesn't concern me. I will not be content. I can hear a voice saying, "If you do it unto the least of these, my brother, you do it unto me."[23]

Sometimes faithful public witness involves organizing in a way that allows the truth of the gospel to shed light on suffering and injustice. Were it not for the significant roles played by church communities and their leaders, the civil rights movement of the twentieth century would not have achieved what it did.

---

22. See Fields, *Montgomery Bus Boycott*.
23. King, "Montgomery Bus Boycott."

Public Witness and Its Reception

To be clear: faithful public witness to the gospel of Jesus does not *require* hostility to be faithful. Some Christians carry this assumption, treating hostility and conflict from others like a badge of honor or virtue. They may point to prophetic figures in Scripture as examples, like Jesus and the biblical prophets who decried injustices in their day and suffered the consequences for it. While true, these prophetic figures strove for *changes* to people's thinking and practice, not to generate hostility for its own sake.

There is a US church with a national reputation for public demonstrations of judgmental messages. They interpret major disasters (like 9/11 and COVID-19) as acts of God's wrath against disobedience. They pass judgment upon all who identify as LGBTQIA+ or who experience gender dysphoria. Their church website domain is "God hates [expletive reference to gay people]." And they believe that the idea "God loves everyone" is "the greatest lie ever told," since God's hatred "runs the current of the scripture, is plainly pronounced, and is vitally important for everyone to know about." The church's greatest claim to fame is its public professions of God's judgment and wrath.

In the very same city, just two miles away, is another church community that is very different. They describe themselves as pro-gay, pro-woman, pro-poor, and pro-immigrant. They emphasize questions over answers, honoring people's distinctive faith journeys, and taking the Bible seriously but not literally. They depict God as one who ultimately calls people to love God with all of themselves and to love their neighbors as themselves. Most of all, they pledge to receive and value all people regardless of gender, race, age, culture, ethnic background, sexual orientation, economic circumstance, family configuration, or ability.

These examples are extreme contrasts, making the comparison instructive. The biggest difference between the two churches' public witnesses is not just their ethical judgments (different as they are), but their characterizations of God. One church portrays God as judgmental, while the other God as accepting. One church emphasizes God's hatred, while the other God's love. One church focuses on differences that exclude, while the other on eradicating differences so as to include. In the end, one church embodies a theology of judgment, and the other a theology of grace.

A church that defines its witness primarily through judgment and hate has no constructive witness to offer, since it is defined primarily through negating. A community that identifies itself by negative claims (who it is not) and God primarily by whom God hates offers the world nothing constructive. It has an inadequate grasp of the expansiveness of God's love and goodness of the gospel.

Faithful witness to the gospel strives to include others more than drawing distinctions that exclude. Thomas Hoyt talks about the practice of testimony, a form of bearing witness, as a communal act. It makes truth known to others so that they may get on board and stand in solidarity.

> In a world where bad news gets more attention than good, a testimony like this tells the truth. It also ties individuals to communities. Although only one person may be speaking at a time, that person's speech takes place within the context of other people's listening, expecting, and encouraging. In testimony, a believer describes what God has done in her life, in words both biblical and personal, and the hands of her friends clap in affirmation. Her individual speech thus becomes part of an affirmation that is shared.[24]

In the same way, faithful witness to the gospel in public settings is at heart a *communal practice*. It strives to gather people into beloved community. It tries to unite people across diverse backgrounds and experiences in affirming a unifying message. Like at Pentecost, bearing public witness strives to gather a community of people who together can say Amen to the promises of Jesus.

The Way of Jesus

Faithful public witness may be informed not only by experiences of the early church but also the ministry and way of Jesus. Most of Jesus' ministry took place in public spaces, widely accessible to large groups of people. In the Gospels, for example, Jesus gathered with people in synagogues, the temple vicinity, and countless outside spaces like the seashore, mountainsides, and deserted places.[25] Even though he gave intentional energy to training twelve followers, Jesus hardly came to start a private club.

When it came to public ministry, furthermore, Jesus taught and embodied a message of divine love and mercy. When asked about the first or

---

24. Hoyt, "Testimony," 94.

25. For example: synagogues: Mark 1:21–29; 3:1–6; 6:1–2; the temple vicinity: 11:15–19; 11:27—13:1; 13:3; 14:49; on the seashore: 2:13–14; 3:9–12; 4:1; 5:1–20; on water: 1:16–20; 4:35–41; 8:13–21; at rivers: 1:9–11; in fields: 2:23–28; on mountains: 3:13–19a; 9:9; 13:3; while traveling: 8:27–30; 9:33; 10:32; deserted places: 1:12–13; 6:32–45; 8:1–10.

greatest commandment, he answered clearly: "you shall love the Lord your God with all your heart, and with all your soul, and with all your mind, and with all your strength." And "You shall love your neighbor as yourself. There is no commandment greater than these" (Mark 12:30–31).[26] Jesus also embodied this message by how he touched lepers, associated with "sinners," plucked grain and healed on the Sabbath, objected to socioeconomic exploitation in the temple, and prioritized divine mercy over purity practices.[27] Although he called out religious leaders who misled and exploited people, at the end of the day the vast majority of people—peasants, sex workers, and sinners of all kinds—loved hanging out with Jesus. That says something. In his interpretation of Scripture and ministry practice, Jesus proclaimed a message that prioritized holistic love for God and justice and mercy for all people. Those who encountered him were deeply attracted to this message of divine grace.

Church communities and people are called to follow Jesus' pattern today. We are called to bear witness to a God known for steadfast love and mercy, made known in Jesus Christ, who calls people to love, who stands with strugglers, and who saves the condemned. Many today have been harmed by experiences of exclusion and condemnation by church communities and people. Christians today are called to challenge and change that reputation, becoming a community who—like Jesus—held a space of grace for society's misfits and outcasts. Inspired by the vision of Pentecost, we are called to bear witness to a God in Christ who by the Holy Spirit calls diverse people together into a community marked by forgiveness and joy.

First Steps: Telling the Story in Public

There are countless approaches and strategies for bearing witness in public spaces. And they vary vastly from context to context. By way of an example, the contexts in which Peter and John (and others in Acts) bore witness are very different than our own: apostasy and blasphemy were punishable crimes in local Jewish communities; the Roman Empire dictated the legality of religious faiths; religious devotion permeated public life; and political

---

26. Matthew's version (22:36–40) adds: "On these two commandments hang all the law and the prophets" (v. 40).

27. For example: Mark 1:40–45; 2:13–17, 23–28; 3:1–6; 7:1–23; 11:15–19; 12:38–44. The language of "mercy" appears in Matthew's version of some of these stories (9:9–13; 12:1–8).

leaders were essentially religious leaders. In these contexts, religious profession was communal (vs. individualistic), holistic (vs. intellectual), and assumed. Further, the message that a Galilean peasant deemed Jewish Messiah yet crucified by Rome is the Savior of the world was a profession of faith that inevitably invited public dishonor in the Roman world. The faith of Jesus faced real challenges in such a world.

Our challenges today are different. For example, in the United States today, religious apathy is strong and growing; impressions of institutionalized religions are negative; Christianity is widely seen as more intolerant than gracious; religious leaders are eyed with increased skepticism; past failures of the church govern present impressions; public displays of faith are unwelcome to some; and cultural individualism considers community to be optional and churches unnecessary. In various ways, the call to bear witness today is both easier and harder than in Acts.

Regardless, the call of Jesus to faithful witness in the world stands. The approaches and strategies are endless. Here are some possible starting points:

- Hold a church meeting or Bible study in a coffee shop, restaurant, pub, or park.
- Organize an event for your church that would directly benefit the larger community.
- Ask local community leaders about churches they see as intentionally active in the community. Learn from what they do.
- Write an editorial to a local news source with insight on a public concern from a faith perspective.
- Wear shirts, hats, or jewelry that reflect your faith with integrity. If someone asks about it, be honest.
- Seek out opportunities for your church to hold worship in alternative, public spaces.
- Hold space in a coffee shop or bar with a sign stating: "Free Prayers."
- Share meaningful verses, quotes, or insights about faith on social media in a way that is charitable, transparent, and constructive for all, including people of other faiths.
- Help your church with public messaging that intentionally expresses welcome to people excluded elsewhere in society—like women, members of the LGBTQIA+ community, refugees, unhoused people, and those with disabilities.

- Set up a table for your church at a local public event and offer free stuff of practical use.
- Talk with local social workers and service agencies to learn more about ways your church could be a better partner with them to address community needs.
- Attend a march or rally in support of a people experiencing discrimination. If appropriate, let it be known you are a person of faith.
- Work to share space with a local humanitarian group in ways that are mutually beneficial.
- Be kind to people in the name of Jesus. Don't be a jerk.
- If people ask you about your faith, speak honestly.

Some of these ideas would work well in your context. Others would flop. Still others may work well with modifications. Other people will have additional suggestions. Some will be more constructive than others. Some suggestions may be unappealing at first but may be worth trying. Others will yield mixed results but will open doors to new relationships. Others will flop but yield good learning. Evaluating each activity with others will offer opportunities for clearer discernment.

Sometimes the only thing to do when it comes to faithful witness in public spaces is simply to try some low-risk things in consultation with others. It may be that the Holy Spirit will show up in an unexpected way.

Conclusion

At the outset, the very first gatherings of church people (after Pentecost) happened in public spaces. As the church grew, it continued to inhabit both public and private spaces, reflecting a movement that was in progress, not entrenched in its final form. In fact, it is no coincidence that the book of Acts distinctively refers to the movement we now call Christianity as "the Way" (*ho hodos*).[28] The language suggests it is more a movement than a creed, more a practice than a building, more a way of life than a particular club. Whatever this movement was, Acts suggests it was a work in progress, led along by God through the Holy Spirit. In these early years, the church migrated, adapted, grew, and evolved. And throughout this time, it continued to enter, inhabit, and influence public spaces.

28. Acts 9:2; 19:9, 23; 22:4; 24:14, 22. See also 16:17; 18:25–26.

Centuries later, the church entered a season of greater leisure and resources. As a result, it built buildings and walls, putting public spaces and arenas on the outside. Although there are many exceptions throughout the world and throughout history, in the Western world that season of leisure has largely continued to this day. As a result, the divide between sacred and secular spaces continues. Even though the church started in public places, church people have worked very hard over the centuries to make it more of a private club.

The patterns of Jesus and of the early church call us to challenge the inertia of the sacred/secular distinction and to bring faithful witness to the gospel of Jesus into the public sphere. Generally, this is a challenging thing for church people. At some level, it always will be. The gospel of Jesus Christ, after all, is counterintuitive to many core values of societies across the globe. But as children of a God who loves this world and its people, we are called to make the distinction between church and public blurrier— even if only by baby steps.

During the summer of 2003, I had an opportunity as part of a culture course in Germany to research the Monday demonstrations that took place in the fall of 1989 in Leipzig. These were a series of peaceful protests against the German Democratic Republic (GDR) of East Germany, which directly contributed to the fall of the Berlin Wall later that year. New to me was learning about the role played by the church.

Throughout the 1980s, the Nikolaikirche (St. Nicholas Church) in Leipzig hosted Monday night prayer meetings. Under the GDR, both religious profession and anti-government thinking were discouraged, sometimes by force. In this climate, the church became a refuge for free thinking, community, and prayer for change. On Monday nights, after an opening prayer from Pastor Christian Führer, people spoke and prayed. And the weekly meetings grew. While at first only a few came, soon dozens and then hundreds gathered.

On Monday September 4, 1989, over a thousand people gathered. That night they began marching in peaceful protest. It continued throughout September, despite dozens of arrests by Stasi police. By September 25, about eight thousand people came. In early October, the Socialist Unity Party leader Erich Honecker issued a "shoot and kill" order for military force to quell the demonstrations. The next Monday gathering, October 9, was fearfully expected to be violent. But that night, as seventy thousand peaceful protesters marched, bearing candles and singing, the roughly eight thousand military personnel in attendance never fired a shot. David Childs calls the success of this nonviolent protest "the miracle of Leipzig." On ensuing Mondays in October, the numbers grew to 120,000 (October 16) and about 300,000 (October 23 and 30). The demonstrations exerted irresistible pressure on the GDR to reform. A month later, on November 9, the Berlin Wall fell.[29]

Although many factors and forces played roles in the change that took place that season in divided Germany, the role played by the church remains an inspiration and reminder of the ways that authentic prayer, gathering, community building, and standing with people may lead to groundbreaking faithful public witness.

Questions for Discussion

1. Read the story of Acts 4:1–22. How is "boldness" (or fearlessness) portrayed?

2. In his book *The House Church in the Writings of Paul*, Victor Branick makes this observation: "Something in the human heart calls for sacred space. We want to point to a spot as the place of God's presence, just as the Israelites could point to their Holy of Holies as the place of God's glory. We want a place where we can shift religious gears and somehow put behind us the perception of divine absence."[30] Do you find this to be true? If so, in what ways is it an unhelpful tendency of church communities today?

3. When you think about Christian witness in the public sphere, what positive and negative examples come to your mind? What impressions of God are conveyed by these examples? What is to be learned?

4. Imagine your church building (if it has one) suddenly burned down, forcing your community to gather for a year or more in a rented public space somewhere in the heart of your local community. What would change?

5. In what ways do you think your faith community could engage the outside world more faithfully?

---

29. Childs, *Fall of the GDR*, 64–76; Schöne, *Peaceful Revolution*; Curry, "We Are the People"; Rinehart, "Peaceful Revolution."

30. Branick, *House Church*, 137.

Resources for Further Exploration

- Church Resources for Public Engagement, from various denominations:
    a. Evangelical Lutheran Church of America, "Publicly Engaged Church," available at https://elca.org/Our-Work/Publicly-Engaged-Church.
    b. Presbyterian Church (U.S.A.) Office of Public Witness, available at https://www.presbyterianmission.org/ministries/compassion-peace-justice/washington/.
    c. United Church of Christ, "How We Serve," available at https://www.ucc.org/what-we-do/.
    d. United Methodist Church, "Advocating for Justice" and "Social Issues," available at https://www.umc.org/en/how-we-serve/advocating-for-justice and https://www.umc.org/en/how-we-serve/social-issues.
    e. United States Conference of Catholic Bishops, "Issues and Actions: Topics," available at https://www.usccb.org/topics.
- Johnson, Luke Timothy. *Prophetic Jesus, Prophetic Church: The Challenge of Luke-Acts to Contemporary Christians.* Grand Rapids: Eerdmans, 2011. Chapter 8 (pp. 166–86).
- Nessan, Craig L. "My Take: Tear Down Magical Walls." *Living Lutheran*, July 9, 2021. https://www.livinglutheran.org/2021/07/my-take-tear-down-magical-walls/.
- Scott, Emily M. D. *For All Who Hunger: Searching for Communion in a Shattered World.* Colorado Springs: Convergent, 2020.
- Walton, Steve. "What Does 'Mission' in Acts Mean in Relation to the 'Powers That Be'?" In *Reading Acts Theologically*, 123–42. The Library of New Testament Series 661. London: T. & T. Clark, 2022.
- Woofenden, Anna. *This Is God's Table: Finding Church Beyond the Walls.* Harrisonburg, VA: Herald, 2020.

Action Steps for Further Consideration

- Read Acts 4:23–31, a story about early believers gathering to pray for boldness in view of opposition. In view of this story, pray for similar fearlessness for your own and your church's public witness.

- The opening story of this book chapter featured church leaders discussing a negative example of public witness, followed by silence to the question: "How might we do something comparable but better?" Brainstorm some constructive examples of more nuanced, faithful public witness today.

- Consult the list of "starting points" (in the section "First Steps: Telling the Story in Public") and identify some that your church community could realistically consider.

- Conduct an inventory of the public messaging your church community has about its mission and message. Invite an outsider or two to eye it and give feedback on what messages you are sending (intentionally or inadvertently) to the world.

- Visit the website of a church that has experimented with inhabiting public spaces, like Humble Walk Church (http://www.humblewalk-church.org/), the Garden Church (https://www.gardenchurchsp.org/), or St. Lydia's Table (https://stlydias.org/). Learn from their stories and experiences and let them spark your imagination for ways that church could look or be different in your setting.

5

Conversing About the Story

> If we really are serious about the "special mission" God has for us—sharing Jesus with everyone—it means paying special attention to who "everyone" is. And that means remembering that everyone is "someone." Each individual is a unique child of God who belongs to a community that is a unique creation of God. Engaging evangelism means getting to know these people, honoring their cultures, and learning to speak their languages. It means being open to what they have to offer and the ways in which we will be changed by our relationship with them.
>
> —Kelly A. Fryer[1]

My internship took place in an inner-city neighborhood. In that neighborhood, an acquaintance of mine used to evangelize on a street corner. On warm evenings, typically with someone, he stood outside broadcasting an invitation to hear about the gospel. He wasn't judgmental or unkind—more like an outgoing salesperson at a shopping mall kiosk than a fire and brimstone preacher.

His approach intrigued me. I thought I would try something similar but less aggressive, to see what happened—even though I was far less outgoing. On a summer evening, I set out a few blocks from my church

---

1. Fryer, *Story Worth Sharing*, 158.

to try it. The first person I met was "Frank." He was hanging about the street corner (likely for business reasons, I now realize). As I approached, he talked with me, hesitantly. Then he asked me for money. I gave him what I had ($20). Taking it, he stared at me, like a scientist eyeing a new species.

After sizing me up, Frank asked sharply: "What are you doing here? Don't you know it's dangerous here for a guy like you?" He told me about a robbery incident that took place recently. "That could happen to you. Now, where are you from?" I pointed at my church. "I'll walk you back. Come on." And without asking, Frank escorted me like a father walking his son home from trouble. I was startled by the offer, but grateful for his care. He certainly knew more about the neighborhood than I did. And he thought my naïveté was an accident waiting to happen. On the walk, Frank told me about himself and the neighborhood. I heard about some of the challenges he and others faced. I learned a lot from listening. We talked for about a half hour. As we arrived at the church, I thanked him and wished him God's blessing. Unfortunately, I never saw him again, in part due to heeding his advice.

Years later, my evangelizing acquaintance reevaluated his practices at that time: "I think there are better ways to build bridges." Evidently, his efforts weren't very fruitful. Meanwhile, my one-time outing was something I'll never forget. I set out to share—and ended up learning how to listen. I learned about the significance of human relationship underneath any talk of the gospel. I have Frank to thank for that.

Faithful witness to the gospel often takes shape through conversation, especially in the context of existing relationships. After all, honest conversations about things that truly matter typically take place more effectively through back-and-forth dialogue, not one-sided monologues. In at least one story in Acts, we see some of these ideals at work—a story of great significance for the unfolding story of worldwide witness as it takes first steps outside the boundaries of Jerusalem.

An Unexpected Encounter: Acts 8:26–40

The encounter between Philip and an Ethiopian is one of the most intriguing stories in Acts. Traditional readings often focus on Philip's activity and experience.[2] But he is hardly the story's primary actor. In fact, the sharing of good news that happens is not due to Philip's initiative at all.

The story begins with a divine prompting in a surreal setting:

---

2. A point made by Dube, "Ethiopian Eunuch."

> 26 Then an angel of the Lord said to Philip, "Get up and go toward the south to the road that goes down from Jerusalem to Gaza." (This is a wilderness road.) 27 So he got up and went. Now there was an Ethiopian eunuch, a court official of the Candace, the queen of the Ethiopians, in charge of her entire treasury. He had come to Jerusalem to worship 28 and was returning home; seated in his chariot, he was reading the prophet Isaiah. (Acts 8:26–28)

The road from Jerusalem to Gaza went through the Judean desert—not a likely spot for an evangelism encounter.[3] The phrase "toward the south" is better translated "at midday," which makes sense for two reasons: first, the location (the road to Gaza) is already quite clear; second, "midday" heightens the encounter's unlikeliness, since it was hardly a prime time for desert encounters in the Middle East.[4] In Beverly Roberts Gaventa's words: "Only God could construct such a scenario."[5]

By this point in Acts, Philip is well known. First appointed to steward food distribution to widows (6:5), he later becomes a leader in sharing the message of Jesus in Samaria (8:4–25). Less known is the man he meets on the way to Gaza: a man from Ethiopia. At this time, many Mediterranean people saw Ethiopia as basically anything south of Egypt. In fact, the story's reference to Candace suggests the man came not from the area we now call Ethiopia (ancient Aksum), but from what today is South Sudan (ancient Nubian kingdom of Meroë).[6] To many ancient Greeks and Romans, Ethiopia was one of the farthest reaches of earth, where people of tall stature lived to old age.[7] In Israel's history and Scriptures, Ethiopians are portrayed more favorably than most peoples.[8] Some of Israel's prophets envisioned

---

3. On whether the region and route truly fit the category of "wilderness" or desert, see Pythian-Adams, "Problem of 'Deserted' Gaza."

4. The phrase *kata mesēmbrian* means "according to the south," which may either refer to geography ("to the south," so the NRSVue) or to the time of day when in the Middle East the sun is at its southernmost point ("at midday," so the NRSVue footnote). Similar language is used elsewhere in Acts to refer to midday (*peri mesēmbrian*, "about midday," 22:6; cf. 26:13).

5. Gaventa, *Acts*, 141.

6. See Yamauchi, "Acts 8:26–40"; also Keener, *Acts*, 2:1550–65.

7. See, for example, Homer, *Odyssey* 1.22–23; Strabo, *Geography* 17.2.1; Heliodorus, *Ethiopian Story*; Herodotus, 2.30–31; 3.19–24; Esth 1:1; 8:9; Ezek 29:10; Zeph 3:10. Herodotus claims the Ethiopians are "the tallest and best-looking people in the world," with distinct laws, precious metal, coffins of crystal, and unanimously wise kings, as well as a people who live to 120 years old (3.19–24). R. Smith, "Ethiopia," 665–68.

8. Ethiopians also had favorable dealings with King Solomon (the Queen of Sheba,

Ethiopians one day streaming to worship Israel's God in Jerusalem (Isa 18:1–7; Zeph 3:8–10). Since this Ethiopian has journeyed such a distance to Jerusalem, he is most likely already a worshiper of Israel's God.

Although later traditions give the man a name (Simeon Bachos), he is never named in Acts. Instead, the story primarily identifies him as a eunuch (8:27, 34, 36, 38, 39). Eunuchs were typically castrated males, often employed as guards in royal harems.[9] Although they had distinctive opportunities for advancement in royal circles, they were widely despised in the Greco-Roman world, associated with unmanliness, gender ambiguity, weakness, and even bad luck.[10] They widely experienced social shame as "unmanly" men who did not cleanly fit either category of male or female.[11]

In ancient Jewish and Christian writings, eunuchs are sometimes portrayed favorably (e.g., Matt 19:12), but their participation in ritual assemblies was restricted (Deut 23:1). As a eunuch and foreigner, this Ethiopian would not have been allowed beyond the court of the gentiles in the temple of Jerusalem.[12] However, most visitors to the temple were restricted to the outer courts of the gentiles and women. Such spatial restrictions to certain groups were common to sacred sites in antiquity. A bit like pilgrims visiting sacred religious sites today, most ancient visitors to religious temples (not just in Jerusalem) did not expect a laid-back welcome to explore every nook and cranny. While the distinctions of the Jerusalem temple seem

---

1 Kgs 10:1–13). The Jewish historian Josephus held that Moses married the daughter of an Ethiopian king (*Antiquities* 2.10.2 §§249–53; cf. Num 12:1) and that the Queen of Sheba was ruler of Egypt and Ethiopia (*Antiquities* 8.6.2 §159; 8.6.5–6 §§165, 175).

9. Philostratus, *Life of the Sophists* 2.12.593. On exceptions to "eunuchs" as exclusively castrated males, see the LXX of Gen 39:1; 40:2; 1 Sam 8:15; Schneider, "εὐνοῦχος, εὐνουχίζω," 766.

10. Julius Caesar counted castration worse than death (*Alexandrian War* 1.70). An essay by Lucian features a speaker opposing an up-and-coming eunuch by contending "that a eunuch was neither man nor woman but something composite, hybrid, and monstrous, alien to human nature" (*Eunuch* 6). See Ovid, *Amores* 2.3; Xenophon, *Cyropaedia* 7.5.61–62; Iamblichus, *Mysteries* 3.10; Catullus, *Carmina* 63.6, 27; Lucian, *Critic* 17; Epictetus, *Discourses* 2.20.17–20; Dio Chrysostom, *Orations* 79.11; Martial, *Epigrams* 3.91; 6.2; 11.75. See also Parsons, *Body and Character*, 123–41.

11. Although there are significant differences between ancient and modern notions of gender and gender consciousness, the eunuch's blurry gender status allows for some parallels with experiences of some LGBTQIA+ people today. See Burke, "Queering Early Christian Discourse," 182.

12. See Acts 21:28. See also Josephus, *Antiquities* 4.8.40 §§290–91; Philo, *Special Laws* 1.324–25; *Yevamot* 8:2; 1QSa II,5–6; 4QMMT B 39–44. However, eunuchs are portrayed as included in an idealized vision of God's assembly in Isaiah 56:3–7 and Wisdom 3:14.

exclusive to many readers today, the Ethiopian's pilgrimage experience to Jerusalem was typical in the ancient world. And Luke nowhere suggests it was a negative experience for the eunuch.[13]

The name "Candace" refers not to a specific individual but to a dynastic title used at this time for many royal consorts or Queen Mothers throughout Nubia, Cush, and Ethiopia.[14] The Candace identified in Acts 8 was likely a royal woman of authority and fame in the larger region. Since this man oversees her "entire treasury," he has access to wealth. Although effectively a slave, the fact he can travel to Jerusalem, be chauffeured by a driver, have a scroll of Isaiah, and be able to read all suggest his wealth and status.

All these factors make the Ethiopian embody a wide range of complex tensions: social status yet shame, court official yet slave, privileged yet excluded, with access yet lack of access, gendered yet gender nonconforming, faithful yet defiled, and insider yet outsider. He defies all the conventional molds of the kind of person to whom Philip might expect to go.[15]

An Unexpected Conversation: Acts 8:26–40 (Continued)

Now that the human characters are identified, the story's main events take place.

> 29 Then the Spirit said to Philip, "Go over to this chariot and join it." 30 So Philip ran up to it and heard him reading the prophet Isaiah. He asked, "Do you understand what you are reading?" 31 He replied, "How can I, unless someone guides me?" And he invited Philip to get in and sit beside him. 32 Now the passage of the scripture that he was reading was this: "Like a sheep he was led to the slaughter, and like a lamb silent before its shearer, so he does not open his mouth. 33 In his humiliation justice was denied him. Who can describe his generation? For his life is taken away from the earth."
>
> 34 The eunuch asked Philip, "About whom, may I ask you, does the prophet say this, about himself or about someone else?" 35 Then Philip began to speak, and starting with this scripture he

---

13. Highlighted by Aymer, "Exotica and the Ethiopian," 537–38.

14. Pliny, *Natural History* 6.186 ("Candace, whose name has passed to queens for many years now"); Keener, *Acts*, 2:1573–79; Khan, "Queen Mother," 67–68. See also Strabo, *Geography* 17.1.54; Dio Cassius, *Roman History* 54.5.4.

15. Highlighted by Spencer, "Ethiopian Eunuch." See also Spencer, *Portrait of Philip*, 158–65.

proclaimed to him the good news about Jesus. 36 As they were going along the road, they came to some water, and the eunuch said, "Look, here is water! What is to prevent me from being baptized?" 38 He commanded the chariot to stop, and both of them, Philip and the eunuch, went down into the water, and Philip baptized him. 39 When they came up out of the water, the Spirit of the Lord snatched Philip away; the eunuch saw him no more and went on his way rejoicing. 40 But Philip found himself at Azotus, and as he was passing through the region he proclaimed the good news to all the towns until he came to Caesarea. (Acts 8:29–40)

Some interpretations treat this as a Christian mission success story, since it ends with a positive response to the good news of Jesus. But the experience is not nearly as conventional or straightforward as it may seem.

Philip the Deacon and the Ethiopian Eunuch, Menologion of Basil II (11th century), public domain, courtesy of Wikimedia Commons

First off, the entire encounter is at God's initiative. Throughout the story, divine agents speak and act to set the main events into motion. It starts with an angel of the Lord telling Philip: "get up and go" to the road leading to Gaza (v. 26). As he arrives, the Spirit tells him: "Go over to this chariot and join it" (v. 29). Finally, after the Ethiopian is baptized, the Spirit of the Lord snatches Philip away to another place (vv. 39–40). Although technically different, the Spirit (Spirit of the Lord) and angel of the Lord work together to serve the same divine purpose.[16] More than most stories in Acts, these divine agents are active and explicitly named many times. All this makes unmistakably clear the divine nature of the story's encounter.

More to the point of this chapter, the story's central activity of witness takes the form of a conversation. However simple a point this is, it is highly instructive. It characterizes faithful witness not as giving speeches and sermons, but as engaging others in a dialogue. Three aspects play significant roles in shaping this conversation the way it is.

First, the conversation's focus is Scripture. As Philip first approaches the chariot, the Ethiopian is reading and pondering the words of Isaiah. Since reading aloud was the norm in antiquity, it was not strange for Philip to overhear the Ethiopian.[17] Philip asks a question that highlights the importance of understanding Scripture: "do you understand what you are reading?" (v. 30). The Ethiopian invites Philip to be a guide as they focus on a specific passage from Isaiah (53:7–8), which draws attention to the experiences of someone humiliated and outcast. The Ethiopian then poses a question with two suggested answers: "About whom . . . does the prophet say this, about himself or about someone else?" (Acts 8:34). Philip, however, does not answer the question so simply. Instead, he shares the good news about Jesus "starting with this scripture" (v. 35). The entire conversation, from start to finish, is a conversation about Scripture.

Second, the conversation revolves around questions. It starts with Philip's opening question: "do you understand what you are reading?" (v. 30). In response, the Ethiopian starts asking questions of his own—several by the story's end:

---

16. This happens often in Acts: different divine agents working together to serve God's overarching purpose. Gaventa observes: "With respect to God, Jesus, and the Spirit, then, they are so identified with one another in Acts that explicitly Trinitarian language seems an inevitable development. Although Luke is not concerned with precisely the same questions that concern later church councils, his story nevertheless moves in a direction that can only be called Trinitarian" (*Acts*, 39).

17. Manguel, *History of Reading*, 41–54; Gamble, *Books and Readers*, 203–5. Gamble observes: "Because authors wrote or dictated with an ear to the words and assumed that what they wrote would be audibly read, they wrote for the ear more than the eye. As a result, no ancient text is now read as it was intended to be unless it [is] also heard, that is, read aloud" (204). Around 400 CE Augustine famously marveled at how Ambrose used to read while "his voice and tongue were silent" (*Confessions* 6.3.3).

Conversing About the Story

- "How can I, unless someone guides me?" (v. 31)
- "About whom, may I ask you, does the prophet say this, about himself or about someone else?" (v. 34)
- "Look, here is water! What is to prevent me from being baptized?" (v. 36)

The Ethiopian is full of questions. In fact, everything he says consists of questions. And it's not just the Ethiopian. The story gives Philip just one instance of direct discourse: his opening question (v. 30). Even though Philip shares the message of Jesus (v. 35), only Philip's opening question is explicitly stated. As a result, the conversation reads like an active dialogue around questions stemming from Scripture, not a sermon from an apostle.[18] The story gives an overall impression that conversation about Scripture and the message of Jesus is not a monologue, but a dialogue fueled by questions.

Third, the conversation is led by the Ethiopian. After Philip's question, the Ethiopian takes over. He invites Philip to join the chariot, directs their attention to a Scripture passage, and asks directly whom Isaiah describes (Acts 8:31–34). In these ways, the Ethiopian sets the terms of discussion and directs Philip how to help. After Philip responds, the Ethiopian suggests a next step, prompted by the appearance of water: "Look, here is water! What is to prevent me from being baptized?" (v. 36). In Greek the question is shorter and pithier (six words), making it more pointed and effectively the story's rhetorical punch line.[19] In an unexpected turn, and for the first time in Acts, baptism is proposed not by the baptizer but by the baptized.

In response, Philip has nothing to say. Verbose as he can be, he is now speechless. Seeing the implied answer of silence, the Ethiopian commands the chariot to stop and enters the water with Philip, where the Ethiopian is baptized. Immediately afterward, Philip is snatched away by the Spirit of the Lord so that the Ethiopian "saw him no more" and went on his way

---

18. Later manuscripts add another verse, after the Ethiopian asks what prevents him from baptism: "And Philip said, 'If you believe with all your heart, you may.' And he replied, 'I believe that Jesus Christ is the Son of God'" (v. 37). Bruce Metzger confidently observes: "Ver. 37 is a Western addition, not found in [the earliest manuscripts]. There is no reason why scribes should have omitted the material, if it had originally stood in the text. . . . Its insertion into the text seems to have been due to the feeling that Philip would not have baptized the Ethiopian without securing a confession of faith" (*Textual Commentary*, 315).

19. *Idou hydōr, ti kōluei me baptisthēnai* ("See water! What keeps me from being baptized?").

(vv. 38–39). Aside from the interventions of divine agents, throughout the story it is the Ethiopian who takes the lead in conversation, action, and response. Far more than Philip, the Ethiopian is the protagonist of the story's central activities from start to finish.[20]

Over the course of this encounter, the Ethiopian becomes a follower of Jesus. Although already devoted to the God of Israel, the experience of this conversation changes him. For one, the Ethiopian is baptized—a trademark response by new followers in Acts (2:41; 8:12–13; 10:48; 16:33–34). For another, the story ends with him "rejoicing," which is typically associated with gentiles who embrace the message of Jesus (8:8; 13:48; 15:31).[21] Finally, the story shows the Ethiopian embarking on a newfound journey on "the way," which is suggestive (or symbolic) language. Among the New Testament writings, only Acts calls the church and its beliefs "the Way" (*hodos*).[22] Not coincidentally, the story of Acts 8:26–40 abounds distinctively in this language:

- Philip travels the way (*hodon*) from Jerusalem to Gaza (vv. 26–27a).
- The Ethiopian asks to be guided in the way: "How can I [understand scripture] unless someone will lead me in the way (*hodēgēsei*)?" (v. 31, my translation).
- After the message of Jesus is shared, the two travel "according to the way" (*kata tēn hodon*) (v. 36).
- The story ends with the Ethiopian traveling the way (*hodon*) rejoicing (v. 39).

By the end of the story, the symbolism about "the way" in which the Ethiopian wishes to be led and on which he comes to travel is unmistakable. Wherever he came from, by the end he is a newfound follower of "the way."

The Significance of Conversation and Questions

Many people associate evangelism with telling a message in a way that requires little active participation from hearers. In other words, many think of it as a one-sided monologue. This is a major reason why so many people

---

20. So Gaventa, *From Darkness to Light*, 102.

21. Joy is also associated in Luke's Gospel with the lost being found: 15:3–7, 8–10, 11–32; 19:9–10.

22. Acts 9:2; 19:9, 23; 22:4; 24:14, 22. See also 16:17; 18:25–26.

have sour impressions of evangelism. It doesn't sound very interpersonal, relational, or sensitive to people's questions and experiences.

That is not the model of witness we find in Acts 8:26–40—nor is it representative of faithful witness in Acts. While public speeches are featured, much of the groundwork for sharing the message of Jesus—in Acts and historically in the early church—often takes shape in other ways, through various forms of interpersonal connections and conversations. The speeches in Acts serve primarily to reflect the content of early witness, not to suggest it happened simply through great speeches by great people.[23] For this reason, the interaction between the Ethiopian and Philip is perhaps more representative of witness "to the ends of the earth" than major speeches by Peter or Paul.

What we find in Acts 8:26–40 is a conversation, centered around questions, focused upon the meaning of Scripture, and guided by the curiosity of the inquirer. Questions fuel healthy conversations; stock answers end conversations. Questions reward curiosity; conventional answers put a lid on curiosity. Conversations engage people in active learning; monologues narrow and limit people's holistic learning. Conversations welcome imagination and creativity; monologue messages put boundaries around imagination and creativity. Conversations invite people to have a hand in creating a story faithful to truth and reality; monologue messages invite people to leave the story primarily to experts.

Under a conversational model, the goal of faithful witness is not to relay a standardized, cookie-cutter message. The goal is to engage people in conversation about faith, spirituality, God, Scripture, and things of ultimate value. Research shows that most adults and teens today who look to God, faith, religion, and/or spirituality for guidance and answers do so with an intentional eye to things like hope, healing, forgiveness, inner peace, truth, purpose, and meaning.[24] And so, conversations about ultimate meaning are, at some level, conversations related to the gospel. Questions like "What

---

23. Justo L. González points out about the witness of the church throughout the early centuries: "In truth, most of the missionary work was not carried out by the apostles, but rather by the countless and nameless Christians who for different reasons—persecution, business, or missionary calling—traveled from place to place taking the news of the Gospel with them" (*Story of Christianity*, 1:30).

24. Barna finds that most teens and adults in the US with interest in spirituality are looking for things like inner peace (37 percent), hope (35 percent), healing (30 percent), forgiveness (30 percent), truth (29 percent), purpose (29 percent), guidance (28 percent), growth (26 percent), meaning (25 percent), and salvation (25 percent). Barna, "Peace, Hope, Healing."

gives you hope?" or "Where does your life find meaning?" can be significant doors to deeply spiritual conversations that engage people where they are and lead to natural connections to the gospel, Scripture, and faith.

During seminary, I served a year as a nursing home chaplain. That's when I met and visited "Don," a fellow who was a bit cantankerous (not just to me). Our conversations were often brief. One day I tried a different approach. After listening to symptoms of his discontent, I asked: "Don, do you feel at peace? . . . with yourself, with others, with God?" He replied sharply: "No!" Suddenly he shared why. He had a conflicted marriage, in which he felt he did not treat his wife well. He had a conflicted life, in which he hurt some of his closest family members. He had a conflicted youth, with figurative scars to show. My question broke open a dam. Soon we were talking about failure, sin, regret, forgiveness, reconciliation, and God. And Don led most of the conversation. He clearly wanted to talk about these things—and with a person of faith. He just needed someone to ask the questions.

John Wesley had a practice of opening small group meetings with the question: "How is it with your soul?"[25] While the language of "soul" is unclear to some, the question is different and deeper than "How are you?" It lends itself to probing more deeply than momentary feelings. Whether or not Wesley's question would work well as is for you, it's the kind of question that may help spark conversations about topics more significant than the weather.

The Significance of Attending to Others

One of the most distinctive aspects of faithful witness in Acts 8:26–40 is how remarkably little initiative Philip takes—and how much he finds himself instead responding to the prompts and questions of others. Beverly Roberts Gaventa notes: "Throughout the story, Philip does what he is told, but very little else."[26] After Philip's initial question, the Ethiopian takes charge: he invites Philip into the chariot, asks him about a Scripture passage, poses a guiding question, asks about baptism, stops the chariot, and orchestrates his baptism. For the lion's share of the story, the Ethiopian leads while Philip simply responds and attends to what his new friend brings up.

In 2021 Barna conducted a poll among Generation Z (Gen Z) respondents (born 1997–early 2010s) asking what traits make for an engaging

---

25. Yoo, "How Is It?"
26. Gaventa, *Acts*, 146.

witness. Among non-Christian respondents, the top two traits associated with an engaging and comfortable witness were:

- "Listens without judgment" (72%)
- "Does not force a conclusion" (57%)

Clearly, Gen Z people appreciate a style of sharing faith that focuses more on open-ended listening than forceful persuasion. The next five top traits identified were as follows:

- "Confident in sharing their own perspective" (49%)
- "Demonstrates interest in other people's story or life" (47%)
- "Good at asking questions" (46%)
- "Allows others to draw their own conclusions" (42%)
- "Aware of the inconsistencies of their own perspective" (30%)[27]

Aside from perhaps the first trait (confidence in one's perspective), all these traits reflect an approach to witness that is more conversational and open-ended than scripted—one that is interested in others' experiences, focused on questions, open to others' answers, and transparent about a faith's inconsistencies. This is a very different approach to evangelism than has conventionally been known to past generations. If the input and experiences of young people today are to be taken seriously, then faithful witness needs to embody intentional listening, questions more than answers, collaborative truth-seeking, and humility. This is an approach that, in many ways, is reflected in the disposition and activity of Philip with the Ethiopian.

And it is not just to the Ethiopian that Philip responds. The entire interaction begins with Philip hearing and heeding the guidance of God. First, an angel of the Lord tells Philip which road to travel (from Jerusalem to Gaza). He is then told by the Spirit to approach and join the Ethiopian's chariot. Unlike other people in Acts who initially object to divine commands—like Ananias (9:13–14) and Peter (10:14)—Philip does not hesitate.[28] These faithful responses put him in a place to engage the Ethiopian in questions and conversation about Jesus. Simply responding to these prompts affords Philip the opportunity to be part of what God is up to in the journey of a traveler returning from Jerusalem.

27. Barna, "What Makes an Engaging Witness."

28. As Ernst Haenchen words it, Philip "scarcely acts at all, and is rather presented as the guided instrument of God" (*Acts*, 316).

The story of Acts 8:26–40 implies a significant theological message: God is already at work in the lives of others before we enter their story. Although we know very little about the Ethiopian's story prior to his encounter with Philip, God is acquainted with it—enough to know just when to lead Philip into it. Presumably, God was actively involved in the Ethiopian's journey long before Philip showed up. And long after the Spirit of the Lord whisks Philip away, God will be actively involved in the Ethiopian's journey afterward. In short, Philip plays a remarkably brief role in the Ethiopian's journey, a journey ultimately guided by and overseen by God.

There is a real message of grace in this: God is the one who leads us into ripe opportunities for witness. Our task is to discern the voice or leading of the Holy Spirit and to respond as faithfully as we can.

The story in Acts makes it sound as if Philip heard a clear, audible voice at each juncture of leading. Maybe he did. Then again, it may not have been an audible voice. For most human beings, identifying God's guidance in hindsight is easy, but doing so in the moment is more difficult. Although Acts portrays Philip's experiences of divine guidance as clear-cut, any historical experiences behind the narrative were likely far less clear. Whereas hindsight is often twenty-twenty, the life of faith for many people feels more often like walking in the fog.

Whatever experiences lie behind it, Acts 8:26–40 relates a story in which God's agents led Philip—and Philip responded. Followers of Jesus today are invited to do the same, however imperfectly.

First Steps: Faithful Witness Within Existing Relationships

In Acts Philip bears witness to someone he just met, but a more practical starting point for most people is existing relationships. Conversations about the gospel, after all, deal with deeply significant and personal beliefs. Most people are unlikely to talk honestly about such things except with those whom they know and trust.

Who are the friends and acquaintances we have, with whom we may hold conversation about significant things? Here are some possible starting points for such conversations:

- Take notice of people's joys and challenges—and ask about them.

- Ask unobtrusive questions about people's hopes, sense of purpose, and faith. Ask out of genuine, open-ended curiosity.
- Take note of the big questions people seem to have about God, evil, suffering, and the world. Invite their working conclusions about these things.
- Offer to pray (not necessarily then and there) for others and their challenges.
- Listen intentionally and reflectively. Demonstrate practices of active listening as a form of care.
- Pay attention to opportunities in conversation that may be "God moments" brought about by the Holy Spirit.
- Admit you don't have all the answers to life's biggest questions.
- Acknowledge the contradictions of Christianity—and the hypocrisy of Christians.
- Be sensitive to how much people do or do not want to hear about your faith.
- Share how your faith helps you navigate daily life.
- Share how the gospel helps you make sense of the world.
- Share how your faith compels you to treat others, especially challenging people.
- Draw connections to stories about Jesus or in Scripture where they naturally happen.
- Do not feel any obligation to resolve discussions unhelpfully.
- Express openness to continuing conversation.

These are merely suggested starting points. Within existing relationships, singular conversations are merely one chapter in a lengthy book. Each conversation can (and should) feel the freedom to go in a direction organic to that conversation.

Most important of all is to take seriously other people's stories and to let the conversation go where it leads. That is essentially what Philip did with the Ethiopian. There was neither a predetermined outcome nor a forced conclusion. Even the resulting baptism is prompted by the Ethiopian's inquiry and interest. All this offers a model of holding loosely to the outcomes or intended directions we may have for a conversation, trusting it will be more fruitful if others are given fullest agency in the process.

We are invited to bring the gospel in various ways into our everyday conversations and interactions with others. In doing so, we are not to center ourselves, our experiences, or our convictions too much. God is already at work in the lives of others. Our work is simply to join that activity and to enhance it, without getting in the way. Eugene Peterson describes the work of ministry this way: "my job is not to solve people's problems or make them happy, but to help them see the grace [already] operating in their lives."[29]

Philip's involvement in Acts 8:26–40 ends abruptly: after the two men emerge from the water, the Spirit of the Lord snatches Philip away (v. 39). Although sudden and unexpected, his departure frees the Ethiopian to start a new course of life without undue influence. While Philip's guidance may have been welcome, the Ethiopian does not need it to follow the way of Jesus. At the Spirit's intervention, Philip gets out of the way of the Ethiopian's journey. That is more instructive than it initially seems. The Ethiopian needs a conversation partner and guide for Scripture and the good news of Jesus. He does not need much more than that. Throughout the story, God leads Philip into a divinely orchestrated encounter—and leads him elsewhere after his work is finished.

Like Philip, we today are called to join where God is active and we are invited, without overstepping or going beyond what is necessary. Especially in past centuries, Christians have engaged in colonialist practices of ministry that have done harm alongside good, by not sufficiently respecting and appreciating the distinctive cultures, identities, and customs of those to whom they have ministered. Faithful witness is not about molding others into our images, but sharing the gospel in a way that invites it to take root in organic new and different ways among others. Our calling is not to control others or the outcomes of the Spirit's work, but to join others in their journeys as we are invited—and to get out of the way when appropriate.

In many ways, the story of Acts 8:26–40 parallels the story of the walk to Emmaus (Luke 24:13–35): a traveler approaches another/others on a journey, asks questions and listens, engages in dialogue about Scripture, shares about the Messiah Jesus, joins with them in a sacramental act (breaking bread, baptism), and disappears. The parallels strongly suggest that Philip's activity with the Ethiopian mirrors the activity of Jesus. That is, the way Philip engages the Ethiopian is not simply a nice approach: it

---

29. E. Peterson, *Contemplative Pastor*, 13.

reflects the ministry and way of Jesus. In bearing witness through a conversational approach like this, Philip follows in the footsteps of the One who first called him to this ministry. We do the same today as we engage in this kind of faithful witness with others.

Conclusion: Joining What God Is Up To

Faithful witness to the gospel may take shape in a conversational way, especially with people whom we already know. As seen in the story of Philip and the Ethiopian, such an approach may be dialogical (vs. monological), collaborative (vs. one-sided), and open-ended (vs. preconceived) in ways that invite the agency of our conversation partners and an openness to the leading of God's Spirit. As we engage in this, we may find the results are neither predictable nor straightforward, and fruitful in ways we do not expect.

My friend "Jane" (now deceased) was a retired chaplain. Her call to ministry came from a conversation with another chaplain, while Jane was in the hospital. That chaplain didn't do much: she talked briefly with Jane, read Scripture, prayed, and left. But it changed Jane. In fact, it inspired her to become a chaplain. She became one of the first female graduates of her seminary and started a nonprofit dedicated to visiting imprisoned people, which she led for decades. To her dying day, Jane credited that chaplain's visit as the first time she heard the call of Jesus to this way of life. Unfortunately, Jane never caught the name of that chaplain, who never learned how significant that day's interaction was. This is often the case with conversations we have about faith: we never know just how significant they may ultimately be.

In the story of Acts 8:26–40, Philip never gets to see where the Ethiopian's journey takes him. Nor do we. Presumably, he returns home, bringing his life-changing encounter to bear upon his witness to the gospel, as later church traditions suggest:

> This man was also sent into the regions of Ethiopia, to preach what he had himself believed. (Irenaeus, *Against Heresies* 3.12.8, about 180 CE)[30]

> Tradition holds that he was the first of the Gentiles to receive the mysteries of the divine word from Philip through revelation, and was the first to return to his native land and preach the Gospel

---

30. Trans. Roberts and Rambaut (*ANF*).

of the knowledge of the God of the universe and the life-giving sojourn of our Savior among [people]. (Eusebius, *Ecclesiastical History* 2.1.13, early fourth century CE)[31]

We do not know the rest of the Ethiopian's story. We only know that, according to Acts, the Ethiopian becomes a first encounter between the message of Jesus and a region associated by many first-century Mediterranean people with the ends of the earth. Whatever happened to the man afterward, the encounter suggests more strongly than any other by this point in Acts: Jesus' promise of worldwide witness (Acts 1:8) is set well into motion with this unconventional man.

We too cannot know the full significance of the interactions and conversations we have with people. We only know that God is active in their lives, present in the encounters and conversations we have, and at work in various ways through us to give people a clearer sense of the way of Jesus.

Questions for Discussion

1. Reread Acts 8:26–40 from the perspective of the Ethiopian. What do you imagine his experience was like? What do you think would have been his primary questions throughout the experience? How does this change your thinking about the events?

2. Think about some of the best conversations you have had with people about God, faith, and things of lasting significance. What traits characterize those conversations? What makes them so memorable and beneficial?

3. What is your reaction to thinking about faithful witness in the context of conversations with others?

4. John Bowen describes evangelism with others as more of an ongoing process than an achievement or singular moment: "The way God draws us is much more relational, and our response is much more devious and messy than [a conventional] image suggests." He suggests finally that "God is not in a hurry"—and neither should we be.[32] How does this help you—to think about faithful witness as a "process," aided by a God who is "not in a hurry"?

31. Trans. Deferrari, *New Fathers of the Church*.
32. Bowen, *Evangelism for "Normal" People*, 3.

5. This chapter proposes that God is already active and at work in the lives of others before we enter. Does this encourage you? Can you think of an experience or interaction that confirms the truth of this idea?

6. As this chapter points out, in Acts 8:26–40 the Ethiopian "defies all the conventional molds of the kind of person to whom Philip might expect to go" (end of "An Unexpected Encounter" section). Who are some similar people for you—people with whom you don't typically interact? Imagine the Spirit tapping you on the shoulder, like Philip, to engage such people in conversation more intentionally.

Resources for Further Exploration

- Acts 8:26–40 in comparison with Luke 24:13–35. Notice the similarities between the two stories: a traveler approaches, a conversational dialogue, and concluding with a sacramental act. How does this make you read Acts 8:26–40 differently?
- Aymer, Margaret. "Exotica and the Ethiopian of Acts 8:26–40: Toward a Different Fabula." *Journal of Biblical Literature* 142.3 (2023) 533–46.
- Barna. "What Makes an Engaging Witness, as Defined by Gen Z." November 10, 2021. https://www.barna.com/research/gen-z-witness/.
- Barreto, Eric. "Commentary on Acts 8:26–39." *Working Preacher*, May, 7 2017. https://www.workingpreacher.org/commentaries/narrative-lectionary/ethiopian-eunuch-baptized/commentary-on-acts-826-39.
- Daubert, Dave. *The Invitational Christian*. Elgin, IL: Day 8 Strategies, 2017. Chapters 5–8.
- Wilson, Brittany E. "'Neither Male Nor Female': The Ethiopian Eunuch in Acts 8.26–40." *New Testament Studies* 60 (2014) 403–22.

Action Steps for Further Consideration

- Consider the friends, relatives, neighbors, and acquaintances you have with whom you could imagine having conversations about God, faith, or significant matters. Pray for these people and their welfare. Look for opportunities for constructive conversation at appropriate times.

- Take stock of how often conversations you are a part of touch upon things related to God, faith, hope, love, compassion, etc.
- Evaluate your listening skills. Are you a good listener? Do others value how well you listen to them? Practice strategies of active listening to be more present for others in conversation.
- Ask someone whom you know what gives them hope or peace in the world today. Share what does this for you, as part of the conversation.

6

Taking the Story to New Places

> Acts forwards a powerful theological argument that faithful unity and ethnic diversity are neither at odds nor mutually exclusive. Luke cannot fathom a world in which our differences are transcended or effaced but narrates a church in which ethnic differences are taken seriously but not allowed to divide us between the inferior and the superior.... What new stories might we craft as we consider the struggles of the church today to make sense of ethnic difference in light of the early days of the church?
>
> —Eric D. Barreto[1]

THERE IS A PREVALENT misconception out there about Acts.

The misconception is that it's essentially a story about the conversion of foreign people ("the heathen") to Christianity. Certainly, a global movement of witness is set into motion. And new people across the world begin to join the movement. But the story is not simply about a conversion among the nations. It is no less a story about the conversion—that is, a radical change of thinking—of the church.

In several stories, like the one spotlighted in this chapter, it is not outsiders to the faith who are dramatically changed to a new way of thinking. Sometimes it is insiders—followers of the Way—who come to a new

---

1. Barreto, "Negotiating Difference," 137.

awareness of God's expansive scope, Christ's saving work, and the Spirit's guidance. It is apostles and communities of Jesus-followers who are challenged to embrace new ways of thinking—and new kinds of people. In stories as these, church leaders like Peter are driven to ask: "who was I that I could hinder God?" (Acts 11:17).

One of the most divisive issues among early Jesus-followers was the inclusion of non-Jewish people (gentiles) into the community of the Way without requiring them first to become fully practicing Jews. This was a high-stakes issue for the earliest community. To appreciate the gravity of the dilemma, as well as the transformative nature of the path down which the Spirit leads, some historical perspective is helpful.

Jews and Gentiles in Historic Perspective

Throughout Israel's history, Jews and gentiles have lived alongside each other, worked together, and exchanged cultural practices with one another. But throughout this history, a distinction between the two has persisted, fueled by both parties and their respective commitments, with varying degrees of strictness at different times and seasons.

The word "gentile" is simply a Jewish word for non-Jews. It comes from references in Scripture to "the nations" (Hebrew *goyim*, Greek *ethnē*), typically meaning "all peoples besides Israel."[2] Non-Jewish people do not call themselves gentiles. The word comes from the people of Israel as language to distinguish themselves from everyone else.

From the formation of Israel to the days of the early church, Jewish views of gentiles vary from extremely positive to rather hostile. Scholars see within the Hebrew Bible (Old Testament) two fundamentally different approaches to non-Jews: one of universalism and coexistence, and another of distinction and separatism. The first approach affirms the humanity of gentiles, accommodates intermingling, and has a vision for all nations revering and being embraced by the God of Israel (see for example Isa 2:3; 56:6–7; Zech 8:20–22). The second approach prohibits intermarriage, restricts eating together, and discourages intermingling based on the belief gentiles are impure and a source of corruption (see for example Deut 7:3–4; Ezra 9:2; Ezek 44:9).[3] These two views are opposite poles of a spectrum, with the ma-

---

2. On language for gentiles in Scripture, see Bertram and Schmidt, "ἔθνος, ἐθνικός," 364–72, esp. 370–72.

3. See also Josephus, *Jewish Wars* 2.10 §150; 4Q271 2.8–12; 4QMMT B 3–9. Even in

jority of people somewhere in the middle. Gravitation toward one pole or the other tended to depend heavily upon Israel's most recent experiences with surrounding nations, whether more peaceable or traumatic.

An example of this is the period after the temple's destruction in 70 CE, when Jewish animosity toward gentiles increased. Rabbinic writings from the ensuing centuries prohibited Jewish women from being alone with gentiles for fear of rape and discouraged all Jews from being alone with gentiles for fear of being murdered (*t. Avod. Zar.* 2.1). While some rabbinic sages prohibited restoring lost property to gentiles (*b. B. Kamma* 113b), others were cynical enough to suggest even "the best of gentiles should be killed" (*y. Qidd.* 4.11,66b). However, these voices are just a few from a very diverse collection, some of which encouraged cooperation with, caring for, and praying for gentiles for the sake of peace (*t. Avod. Zar.* 1.3).[4] Nonetheless, these voices reflect a low point in Jew-gentile relations due to several painful conflicts, including the destruction of Jerusalem. This was the general era in which Luke-Acts was written.

Gentiles also had varying views of Jews, spurred on by their distinctive patterns and practices. Many Greek and Roman writers considered Jews to be unfriendly (*misoxenon*).[5] Others stereotyped Jews as lazy (for not working on the Sabbath), picky eaters (for their dietary practices), and unpatriotic (for not revering Roman deities).[6] In the words of the Roman historian Tacitus, writing in the early second century CE: "The Jews regard as profane all that we hold sacred; on the other hand, they permit all that we abhor. . . . [The] customs of the Jews are base and abominable and owe their persistence to their depravity."[7] Legally, the Roman Empire exercised tolerance of Jewish religious practices, since they were part of an ancient religion (a *religio licita*).[8] But individual Romans had their own views, which were often uninformed, unfavorable, and prejudiced.

---

the most separatist Jewish sources, whether gentiles are fundamentally impure is typically unclear or ambiguous, but some rabbinic sources suggest that a gentile who converts to Judaism must undergo purification (*Pesahim* 8.8; *Qiddushin* 3.12,64d; *Yevamot* 41a). See Ben Shahar, "Jewish Views of Gentiles."

4. See also *Gittin* 3.13-14; *Avodah Zarah* 2.1. Cf. *Menahot* 43b:17-18.

5. Hecataeus in Diodorus Siculus 40.3.4; Josephus, *Against Apion* 2.11 §§121-24; Tacitus, *Histories* 5.5.

6. Josephus, *Against Apion* 2.2 §§8-27; 2.6 §§65-78; Juvenal, *Satires* 14.96-106. See J. Daniel, "Anti-Semitism"; Littman, "Antisemitism."

7. Tacitus, *Histories* 5.4-5 (trans. Moore).

8. Smallwood, *Jews Under Roman Rule*, 539-45. For example, although Julius Caesar

Throughout Israel's history, non-Jewish people have been allowed and incorporated into the community by various means (intermarriage, service, circumcision). Even so, views of newcomers varied. Ruth, for example, relinquished her people even after her husband's death to remain loyal to her mother-in-law's people, yet continued to be identified as a Moabite and a foreigner (Ruth 2:10; 4:5). For males, circumcision was the most concrete sign of conversion to the Jewish faith.[9] At times, Jewish rulers obligated some non-Jewish inhabitants of their lands to be circumcised, though it seems to have been motivated more by interests in religious homogeneity than in spreading Judaism per se.[10] There is no clear evidence of an organized effort by Jews to convert gentiles to Judaism for its own sake.[11]

And yet, some gentiles were attracted to Judaism and its practices. A few first-century examples show this. Queen Helena of Adiabene, along with her son, converted to the Jewish faith and relocated to Jerusalem (Josephus, *Antiquities* 20.2.1—4.2 §§17–96).[12] Fulvia, the wife of Saturninus (one of Emperor Tiberias's entourage), embraced Jewish devotion to the extent of sending purple and gold to the temple in Jerusalem (Josephus, *Antiquities* 18.3.5 §82). Others accepted Jewish belief and practice more moderately or partially. Philo, for example, conjectures that the Roman governor Patronius refrained from introducing a statue of Emperor Caligula into the Jerusalem temple because Patronius admired aspects of the Jewish faith (Philo, *Leg. Gaius* 33.243–53). Gentiles like these, who respected and observed Judaism in certain ways without becoming full proselytes or converts were often called "God fearers" or "God worshipers."[13] This language is used to describe Cornelius at his first appearance in Acts (10:1–2).

---

banned many associations (*collegia*) in 64 BCE, he explicitly allowed Jews to build synagogues, maintain property, send envoys to Jerusalem unmolested, and to be exempt from court summonses on the Sabbath (Smallwood, *Jews Under Roman Rule*, 135).

9. Gen 17:9–14; 34:13–17; Judith 14:10; Josephus, *Antiquities* 13.9.1 §§257–58; 13.11.3 §318; 20.7.1 §139.

10. The second century BCE Hasmonean kings John Hyrcanus and Aristobulus I (the Philhellene), for example, required this of some Idumeans and Itureans, respectively, forcing them to be circumcised—and the Idumeans to heed Jewish laws—if they were to remain on their lands (Josephus, *Antiquities* 13.9.1 §§257–58; 13.11.3 §318).

11. Goodman, "Jewish Proselytizing"; Ben Shahar, "Jewish Views of Gentiles," 644–45.

12. On conversion by non-Jews to Judaism in the Second Temple period, see Feldman, "Conversion to Judaism in Classical Antiquity."

13. Greek *theosebeis* or *theophoboi* (or *phoboumenoi ton theon*). The language is found on mortuary inscriptions and dedications, in addition to appearing in Acts (10:1–2;

As history shows, gentiles were ultimately included into early church communities, but not without significant tensions and dissension. It is not an understatement to say that their inclusion—and more specifically the terms on which it might take shape—provoked a crisis of identity and self-definition for the early church. After all, at the outset the early church understood itself as a fresh initiative within the faith of Israel—not a separate religious tradition.

Acts 10:1—11:18: "Even to the gentiles..."

The story of Acts 10:1—11:18 is what Beverly Roberts Gaventa calls "the climactic moment of the first half of Acts."[14] Its length, elaborateness, moments of divine intervention, and number of repetitions all imply the story's profound significance for the narrative. At 66 verses, the story represents about 15 percent of Acts. It's also one of just two events in Acts to be recalled and repeated twice (10:1–48; 11:1–18; 15:7–9).[15] The effect of these narrative aspects draws increased attention to the events at hand as significant for the overall story of Acts.

Although long, the story is a united piece. To consider only part would not suffice. For this reason, the text is reproduced in segments below:

> 1 In Caesarea there was a man named Cornelius, a centurion of the Italian Cohort, as it was called. 2 He was a devout man who feared God with all his household; he gave alms generously to the people and prayed constantly to God. 3 One afternoon at about three o'clock he had a vision in which he clearly saw an angel of God coming in and saying to him, "Cornelius." 4 He stared at him in terror and said, "What is it, Lord?" He answered, "Your prayers and your alms have ascended as a memorial before God. 5 Now send men to Joppa for a certain Simon who is called Peter; 6 he is lodging with Simon, a tanner, whose house is by the seaside." 7 When the angel who spoke to him had left, he called two of his slaves and a devout soldier from the ranks of those who served

---

13:16, 26, 50; 16:14). Ben Shahar, "Jewish Views of Gentiles," 644. Jacob Jervell argues that virtually all non-Jewish conversions in Acts are among gentiles rightly categorized as Godfearers ("Church of Jews and Godfearers").

14. Gaventa, *Acts*, 162.

15. The other event is the conversion or reorientation of Saul/Paul (9:1–18; 22:3–21; 26:7–18). Within Acts 10:1—11:18, Daniel Marguerat finds four accounts of Cornelius's vision (10:1–6, 22, 30–32; 11:13–14) (*Actes*, 366).

> him, 8 and after telling them everything he sent them to Joppa. (Acts 10:1–8)

From the outset, Cornelius is portrayed as honorable, devout, and generous. He is first "a devout man who feared God," using classic language for non-Jews committed to the Jewish faith. As a devout man in a patriarchal world, his household shares his devotion. Further, he regularly and generously gives alms and prays "constantly to God." Both traits (almsgiving, prayer) are hallmark indications of faithfulness in Jewish tradition.[16] His alms go "to the people"—that is, Jews—just like another centurion earlier in Luke-Acts who built a synagogue because "he loves [the Jewish] people" (Luke 7:5). All these traits of Cornelius would have challenged widespread Jewish stereotypes of gentiles as nothing but idolaters. All told, Cornelius is a devout, upstanding, gentile worshiper of Israel's God.

Even more, Cornelius is a ranking officer of the Roman army. Literary and archaeological evidence suggests soldiers and infantry auxiliaries were stationed in Caesarea throughout the first century and at this time.[17] As a centurion, Cornelius was most likely a Roman citizen who held authority over sixty to eighty men.[18] He is a man of imperial authority. And his authority is entirely bound up with what many Jews saw as an oppressive, foreign, imperial power. In that sense, Cornelius represents not only gentiles but an imperial oppressor. By sociopolitical standards, he is "the enemy" for Jews. But his prayers and alms have caught God's attention. And to him an angel of the Lord appears to give instruction, which Cornelius faithfully heeds by sending people to Joppa.

> 9 About noon the next day, as they were on their journey and approaching the city, Peter went up on the roof to pray. 10 He became hungry and wanted something to eat, and while it was being prepared he fell into a trance. 11 He saw the heaven opened and something like a large sheet coming down, being lowered to the ground

---

16. See Tob 12:8; Matt 6:2–6; 1 Pet 4:7–11; Didache 15:4; 2 Clem. 16:4.

17. Josephus, *Antiquities* 19.9.1–2 §§356–65; Keener, "Acts 10." Skeptics of this are Haenchen (*Acts*, 360) and Hans Conzelmann (*Acts*, 81). Keener argues: "It is virtually impossible lexically to deny that Josephus refers to soldiers in Caesarea during this time" (*Acts*, 2:1735).

18. Keener, *Acts*, 2:1734–44. Although "centurion" implies one hundred soldiers, a more realistic estimate is sixty to eighty men. Legions (vs. auxiliaries) did not exist in Judea at this time. Most commentators associate the "Italian cohort" in the story with the *Cohors II Italica civium Romanorum*, whom Josephus suggests was made up primarily of Syrians (*Jewish War* 3.4.2 §66). So C. K. Barrett, *Acts*, 499; Fitzmyer, *Acts*, 449.

> by its four corners. 12 In it were all kinds of four-footed creatures and reptiles and birds of the air. 13 Then he heard a voice saying, "Get up, Peter; kill and eat." 14 But Peter said, "By no means, Lord, for I have never eaten anything that is profane or unclean." 15 The voice said to him again, a second time, "What God has made clean, you must not call profane." 16 This happened three times, and the thing was suddenly taken up to heaven. (Acts 10:9–16)

Since Joppa is over thirty miles from Caesarea, Cornelius's men make quick work of the trip, likely traveling some that night. Meanwhile, the next day Peter receives his own vision while praying.[19] With divine authority, the vision tells Peter to "kill and eat."[20] Although the story's description is rather vague about what kinds of animals appear ("all kinds of four-footed creatures and reptiles and birds of the air"), Peter's reaction shows some are unclean for Jews according to the Torah: "By no means, Lord, for I have never eaten anything that is profane or unclean" (Acts 10:14). Peter's objection recalls the prophet Ezekiel's refusal to eat impurely prepared meat (Ezek 4:14). In Ezekiel's case, God grants an alternative. In Acts, God grants no alternative: "What God has made clean, you must not call profane" (10:15). In fact, God's response uses verbs that directly counter Peter's objection:

> Peter: I have never eaten anything that is profane (*koinon*) or unclean (*akatharton*). (Acts 10:14)

> God: What God has made clean (*ekatharisen*), you must not call profane (*koinou*). (Acts 10:15)

Peter assumes he knows what is clean and unclean. But God disagrees. As the story points out, the vision happens to Peter three times, suggesting its heightened significance—as well as Peter's stubborn need for its reiteration.

> 17 Now while Peter was greatly puzzled about what to make of the vision that he had seen, suddenly the men sent by Cornelius appeared. They were asking for Simon's house and were standing by the gate. 18 They called out to ask whether Simon, who was called Peter, was staying there. 19 While Peter was still thinking about

---

19. Several parallels tightly connect the experiences of Cornelius and Peter in 10:1–8, 9–16 [17–23]: both receive a vision at a specific time of day (vv. 3, 9) in association with a time of prayer (vv. 2–3, 9–10), engage the vision in dialogue (vv. 4–6, 13–15), receive specific instructions (vv. 5–6, 15, 20), address the divine agent as "Lord" (vv. 4, 14), and ultimately respond faithfully (vv. 7–8, 21–24).

20. The language "He saw the heaven opened" reflects language of divine revelation in Scripture. See Ps 78:23; Isa 24:18; 64:1; Ezek 1:1; Matt 3:16; Rev 19:11.

the vision, the Spirit said to him, "Look, three men are searching for you. 20 Now get up, go down, and go with them without hesitation, for I have sent them." 21 So Peter went down to the men and said, "I am the one you are looking for; what is the reason for your coming?" 22 They answered, "Cornelius, a centurion, a righteous and God-fearing man who is well spoken of by the whole Jewish people, was directed by a holy angel to send for you to come to his house and to hear what you have to say." 23 So Peter invited them in and gave them lodging.

The next day he got up and went with them, and some of the brothers and sisters from Joppa accompanied him. 24 The following day they came to Caesarea. Cornelius was expecting them and had called together his relatives and close friends. 25 On Peter's arrival, Cornelius met him and, falling at his feet, worshiped him. 26 But Peter made him get up, saying, "Stand up; I am only a mortal." 27 And as he talked with him, he went in and found that many had assembled, 28 and he said to them, "You yourselves know that it is improper for a Jew to associate with or to visit an outsider, but God has shown me that I should not call anyone profane or unclean. 29 So when I was sent for, I came without objection. Now may I ask why you sent for me?" (Acts 10:17–29)

At first Peter is baffled by the vision—a point duly emphasized by several colorful verbs like "greatly puzzled" (*diēporei*).[21] Suddenly the Spirit speaks directly: "Look, three men are searching for you. Now get up, go down, and go with them without hesitation, for I have sent them." The language "Get up" and "go" is used earlier in Acts for divine instructions (8:26; 9:11, 15). The phrase "without hesitation" adds urgency. And the explanation "for I have sent them" makes clear who is orchestrating the events about to happen.

At Peter's request, the travelers explain why they have come, largely repeating past events. They add that Cornelius is praised "by the whole Jewish people" and wishes "to hear what you have to say." Peter hosts them that night. The next day they set out for Caesarea, accompanied by some of Joppa's believing community. Cornelius prepares by gathering relatives and close friends, who constitute "many" (v. 27). When Peter arrives, Cornelius's initial gesture ("falling at his feet, worshiped him") is likelier an act

---

21. Along with "greatly puzzled" (*diēporei*) (v. 17), "thinking through" (*dienthumoumenou*) (v. 19), and "hesitating" (*diakrinomenos*) (v. 20) all begin with the same prefix (*dia-*), an additive that subtly intensifies the activities described.

of excessive reverence than idolatry.[22] At seeing the gathered assembly, Peter reiterates how improper it is for devout Jews to associate with gentiles, something his audience would already have known.[23] Peter then recalls language from his vision: "God has shown me that I should not call anyone profane [*koinon*] or unclean [*akatharton*]" (v. 28). This shows clearly that Peter associates the vision's animals with the people before him, interpreting the vision to mean God alone defines what and who is clean—and God is now pushing Peter toward redefined boundaries.

> 30 Cornelius replied, "Four days ago at this very hour, at three o'clock, I was praying in my house when suddenly a man in dazzling clothes stood before me. 31 He said, 'Cornelius, your prayer has been heard, and your alms have been remembered before God. 32 Send therefore to Joppa and ask for Simon, who is called Peter; he is staying in the home of Simon, a tanner, by the sea.' 33 Therefore I sent for you immediately, and you have been kind enough to come. So now all of us are here in the presence of God to listen to all that the Lord has commanded you to say."
>
> 34 Then Peter began to speak to them: "I truly understand that God shows no partiality, 35 but in every people anyone who fears him and practices righteousness is acceptable to him. 36 You know the message he sent to the people of Israel, preaching peace by Jesus Christ—he is Lord of all. 37 That message spread throughout Judea, beginning in Galilee after the baptism that John announced: 38 how God anointed Jesus of Nazareth with the Holy Spirit and with power; how he went about doing good and healing all who were oppressed by the devil, for God was with him. 39 We are witnesses to all that he did both in Judea and in Jerusalem. They put him to death by hanging him on a tree, 40 but God raised him on the third day and allowed him to appear, 41 not to all the people but to us who were chosen by God as witnesses and who ate and drank with him after he rose from the dead. 42 He commanded us to preach to the people and to testify that he is the one ordained by God as judge of the living and the dead. 43 All the prophets testify about him that everyone who believes in him receives forgiveness of sins through his name." (Acts 10:30–43)

---

22. Cf. Acts 14:8–18. The word for "worshiped" (*prosekunēsen*) literally means "bent the knee," which is closer to the meaning of Cornelius's act here.

23. It was not contrary to the Torah for Jews to associate with gentiles, and Peter's word "improper" (*athemitos*) may equally be translated "unconventional" or "untraditional." Still, careful observance of dietary practices made it awkward and a piety risk to engage in many forms of association.

Besides recapping earlier events, Cornelius's words (vv. 30–33) largely serve to introduce Peter's speech, characterizing it as a solemn assembly ("in the presence of God") for hearing what "the Lord has commanded" Peter to say (v. 33). Peter begins with the emphatic claim: "I truly understand that God shows no partiality." This is not a new idea in Scripture (Deut 10:17).[24] But Peter gives it a more specific angle by claiming it here and now. As he soon clarifies, here the idea means that anyone from "any people" (*ethnei*) who reveres God and practices righteousness is acceptable to God (v. 35).[25] Peter's opening phrase "I truly understand . . ." suggests an arrival at a decisive conclusion of spiritual and theological discernment.

Thereafter Peter summarizes the ministry, death, and resurrection of Jesus, culminating in an invitation to faith with the promise of the forgiveness of sins. The response to his message catches Peter by surprise:

> 44 While Peter was still speaking, the Holy Spirit fell upon all who heard the word. 45 The circumcised believers who had come with Peter were astounded that the gift of the Holy Spirit had been poured out even on the gentiles, 46 for they heard them speaking in tongues and extolling God. Then Peter said, 47 "Can anyone withhold the water for baptizing these people who have received the Holy Spirit just as we have?" 48 So he ordered them to be baptized in the name of Jesus Christ. Then they invited him to stay for several days. (Acts 10:44–48)

Mid-speech, Peter is interrupted by the Holy Spirit's arrival. Nowhere else in Luke-Acts does the Holy Spirit fall upon people prior to baptism. Those upon whom the Spirit falls speak in tongues, confirming the Spirit's presence and creating parallels with the earlier event of Pentecost. The Jewish believers are "astounded"—language earlier associated with miracles—that "even on the gentiles" is the Spirit poured.[26] Peter's response is a logical conclusion to such a miraculous event: "Can anyone withhold the water for baptizing these people . . . ?" (v. 47). The scene concludes with Peter and

---

24. In the Hebrew Bible, the concept often refers to God's impartiality among socioeconomic differences. See Lev 19:15; Ps 82:2; Sir 35:15–16. On God having no partiality (*prosōpolēmptēs*, lit. "face taker") in the New Testament, see Rom 2:11; Col 3:25; Eph 6:9; Jas 2:1, 9.

25. The word used for "people" (*ethnos*) is often translated "nation" or more specifically "gentile."

26. In Greek, the phrase "even on the gentiles" (*kai epi ta ethnē*, v. 45) is placed at the front (cf. 11:18). On "astounded" language (*exestēsan*) in association with other miracles, see Acts 2:7, 12; 8:9, 11, 13; 9:21; 12:16.

his companions not only baptizing Cornelius and his guests, but also staying with them for several days. This suggests the inclusion of gentiles into the community involves more than just a baptism: it marks the start of an enduring, reciprocal relationship of hospitality and community.

The final segment of the story (11:1–18) recapitulates the story's events, but in a new context (Jerusalem), with a different audience (Jewish believers), and in response to a more pointed question.

> 1 Now the apostles and the brothers and sisters who were in Judea heard that the gentiles had also accepted the word of God. 2 So when Peter went up to Jerusalem, the circumcised believers criticized him, 3 saying, "Why did you go to uncircumcised men and eat with them?" 4 Then Peter began to explain it to them, step by step, saying, 5 "I was in the city of Joppa praying, and in a trance I saw a vision. There was something like a large sheet coming down from heaven, being lowered by its four corners, and it came close to me. 6 As I looked at it closely I saw four-footed animals, beasts of prey, reptiles, and birds of the air. 7 I also heard a voice saying to me, 'Get up, Peter; kill and eat.' 8 But I replied, 'By no means, Lord, for nothing profane or unclean has ever entered my mouth.' 9 But a second time the voice answered from heaven, 'What God has made clean, you must not call profane.' 10 This happened three times; then everything was pulled up again to heaven. 11 At that very moment three men, sent to me from Caesarea, arrived at the house where we were. 12 The Spirit told me to go with them and not to make a distinction between them and us. These six brothers also accompanied me, and we entered the man's house. 13 He told us how he had seen the angel standing in his house and saying, 'Send to Joppa and bring Simon, who is called Peter; 14 he will give you a message by which you and your entire household will be saved.' 15 And as I began to speak, the Holy Spirit fell upon them just as it had upon us at the beginning. 16 And I remembered the word of the Lord, how he had said, 'John baptized with water, but you will be baptized with the Holy Spirit.' 17 If then God gave them the same gift that he gave us when we believed in the Lord Jesus Christ, who was I that I could hinder God?" 18 When they heard this, they were silenced. And they praised God, saying, "Then God has given even to the gentiles the repentance that leads to life." (Acts 11:1–18)

Not everyone receives news of the events in Acts 10:1–48 positively. The interaction of 11:1–18 starts with criticism of Peter, specifically his associating with gentiles ("uncircumcised men"). The believers in Jerusalem "criticize" (*diakrinonto*) Peter, mimicking an activity earlier discouraged by the Spirit: "go . . . without hesitating (*diakrinomenos*)" (10:20). The parallel strongly suggests their criticism contradicts the will of the Holy Spirit. In response, Peter briefly reviews past events with a focus on his own experiences. In his conclusion, he draws connections to opening events of Acts: Pentecost (11:15, cf. 2:1–4) and Jesus' words (11:16, cf. 1:5).

Peter closes with a decisive rhetorical question:

> "If then God gave them the same gift that [God] gave us when we believed in the Lord Jesus Christ, who was I that I could hinder God?" (11:17)

Peter ends his words with a question similar to that in chapter 10:

> "Can anyone withhold the water for baptizing these people who have received the Holy Spirit just as we have?" (10:47)

Both questions highlight the concern of getting in God's way. They are two among several times in Acts that the question surfaces at critical moments of discernment (5:39; 15:10). Collectively, these questions suggest human beings—especially religious leaders—are prone to get in the way of God's purposes, and so "kick against the goads" (26:14).[27] Meanwhile, the presence and activity of God's Spirit make clear: God is doing something unexpected; human beings best not unknowingly get in the way.

Peter's summary and question silence his audience. In response, they verbalize the central discovery of the entire episode: "Then God has given even to the gentiles the repentance that leads to life" (11:18). In Greek, the phrase "even to the gentiles" (*kai tois ethnesin*) is placed at the front, emphasizing it (like in 10:45). Most importantly, their conclusion expands the scope of what has happened with Cornelius and his companions to *all* gentiles.

Prioritizing Those Outside: "God Shows No Partiality"

As Craig Keener points out, the issues addressed by Acts 10:1—11:18 "were burning ones."[28] In Luke's day, in the wake of the first Jewish-Roman war

---

27. Paul's quotation in Acts 26:14 of a proverb from Euripides (*Bacchae* 795) reflects a widespread sentiment from Greek tragedy, namely, that it is an act of human folly to try resisting the gods. See Euripides, *Iphigenia in Tauris* 1396; Pindar, *Pythian* 2.94–96; Aeschylus, *Agamemnon* 1624.

28. Keener, *Acts*, 2:1728.

(66–74 CE), relations between Jews and gentiles—specifically *Roman* gentiles—were at a peak point of hostility. As a centurion, Cornelius represented Roman gentiles distinctively. In short, he was a poster boy of the evil empire.

In the late first century, there were active conversations—and abundant disagreement—among early Christians about several core community issues:

- Table fellowship: with whom should we associate—and in what specific ways?[29]
- Baptism: on what terms may someone receive it?
- Circumcision: is it essential to being a follower of Jesus?

All these issues are actively in play in Acts 10:1—11:18. And they are not easily distinguished.

The wonder of this story is not that a gentile becomes devoted to the Jewish faith. That was happening long beforehand—and was already the case with Cornelius. The real wonder is that he is fully included into the community of Jesus-followers without requiring circumcision, which at this time was the most prevalent (and tangible) sign of conversion to Judaism. In forgoing that requirement for gentiles, the early church was making a decisive break from a prevalent religious convention. Cornelius's embrace by Jewish church representatives (and the Holy Spirit) to be baptized and join their fellowship—without circumcision—endorses uncircumcised gentiles like him to be fully included in all church communities.

The issue here is much bigger than a gentile's conversion. It marks a fuller conversion (change) of the church in relation to outsiders. The change marks a shift from a disposition of boundary preservation to a more adaptive engagement with surrounding peoples. And in the process, two parties traditionally at enmity (or at least in tension) with one another are brought closer together. In doing so, both parties are compelled to loosen their grips on historic animosities, grievances, and restrictions that otherwise set up barriers.

This story invites reflection by church communities today about the kinds of people often barred from full participation due to conventional practices, cultural norms, and unchecked biases. In the first century, most Jewish communities of the Way likely saw themselves as "welcoming" to non-Jews, even as they expected conventional marks of Jewish conversion

---

29. See Gal 2:11–14; 1 Cor 5:11. Cf. Acts 10:28; 11:3.

like circumcision. In eliminating this barrier, the early church made a bold and hospitable move that was radical for their day—and we are grateful for it. As David Tiede comments on this text: "Before we are consulted, God is already accepting others as they are."[30]

The Spirit's Initiative

These changes were not minor for early church communities—nor did they take shape easily. But according to Acts they were Spirit led, Spirit initiated, and Spirit facilitated. Writing about Acts 10:1—11:18, Beverly Roberts Gaventa points out:

> The role played by the Holy Spirit in this episode is remarkable, since it is the Spirit who finally forces Peter to move toward baptism for Cornelius and his household. Theological efforts to restrict the Spirit's role to something predictable stumble over this passage, in which Cornelius makes no profession of faith or repentance and Peter does not convey the Spirit through the laying on of hands. The spirit indeed blows where it wishes (see John 3:8).[31]

By Luke's telling of the tale, in no way whatsoever do Peter, the church in Jerusalem, or other leaders *decide* to embrace gentiles as full-fledged members of the Way. Church leaders and representatives come to discern this only by the strong hand of Someone outside themselves.

Although it is conventional to speak of this story as a story of conversion—whether of Cornelius and his associates, or of Peter and early church leaders—this shorthand expression runs the risk of overshadowing who the primary actor in the story is: the Holy Spirit. From start to finish, Luke's story makes clear that the Spirit is at the helm in efforts to include and embrace gentiles.[32] Even in word count, references to the Spirit easily appear more times in this story than any other in Acts.[33] Throughout the story, the Holy Spirit is undoubtedly the primary mover and shaker. The

---

30. Tiede, "Conversion of the Church," 46.

31. Gaventa, *Acts*, 174.

32. See, for example, how frequently God and the Spirit are identified as actors in Peter's retelling (11:5–17) and in the closing verses: "'If then God gave . . . , who was I that I could hinder God?' . . . And they praised God, saying, 'Then God has given . . .'" (vv. 17–18).

33. Eight times (10:19, 38, 44–45, 47; 11:12, 15–16). By comparison, the story of Pentecost refers to the Holy Spirit five times (2:4, 17–18, 33, 38).

upshot of this is an authoritative confirmation of the point: God has indeed welcomed gentile believers, uncircumcised and all, as equals alongside Jews—and is compelling the church to follow suit.

The Spirit's prominence at this critical juncture in Acts is not a minor point. Nor is it a minor point for consideration today. The story portrays the Holy Spirit as a significant changemaking agent for critical decisions and new paths. Where communities of the Way are called to enter unknown spaces or embrace unconventional patterns, the Spirit leads God's people to engage in intentional discernment to respond faithfully. However important human efforts are for major change, it is the Spirit's presence and leading that give the conviction, confidence, and clarity needed for such bold initiatives.

The Call to Spiritual Discernment

Sensing (and heeding) the guidance of the Holy Spirit is an act of spiritual discernment. Spiritual discernment is simply recognizing and responding to the presence and activity of God, in both the ordinary moments and the larger decisions of life. It is a practice both for individuals and for communities. It is a process by which people arrive at greater clarity about where God is active, what God is doing, and how God is leading. It is what Eugene Peterson refers to as "praying with [our] eyes open."[34]

In various stories in Acts, especially Acts 10:1—11:18 and 15:1–28, several considerations for spiritual discernment become clear.[35] These are the activities that seem to influence and inform the discernment of Jesus communities most of all:

1. Testimonies of Experience

    - In Acts 10-11, it is primarily events of divine leading (visions, voices, circumstances, gatherings, anointings) that prompt the entire series of events—and the conclusions drawn. Elsewhere in Acts, various events prompt intentional discernment (6:1–6; 15:1–29; 16:6–10).

---

34. E. Peterson, *Contemplative Pastor*, 76–92. This language refers to a chapter title, which embodies how Annie Dillard approached life and spirituality, in contrast to John Calvin who (according to Peterson) largely remained focused on his books.

35. For more on this topic, see Walton, "Deciding About Deciding."

- Today this takes the basic form of paying attention—to events, circumstances, happenings, and developments in our daily lives and in the world around us. The basic question "What is God up to?" is the focal question.

2. Scripture

   a. In Acts 10–11, Scripture is a regular dialogue partner for Peter, at first in support of conventional patterns (10:13–15), but later scriptural phrases like "God shows no partiality" take on a new understanding (10:34)—as does a teaching of Jesus' (11:16). Scripture plays a significant role in other junctures of discernment in Acts (15:15–17).

   b. Today engagement with Scripture is a natural dialogue partner for discernment, not only historically informed reading but also contemplative reading. Rowan Williams points out: "Bible-reading is an essential part of the Christian life because *Christian life is a listening life*. Christians are people who expect to be spoken to by God."[36]

3. People and Community

   - In Acts 10–11, although experiences and events set discernment in motion, it is only at gatherings with other people that such discernment becomes widely embraced and its conclusions ratified. At gatherings with both Cornelius's people and with leaders in Jerusalem, decisive conclusions of discernment come forth (10:47; 11:17–18). Elsewhere in Acts, gatherings of leaders for discernment are a regular practice (1:15–26; 6:1–6; 15:1–29).

   - Today this plays out primarily in Christian community, but also in meeting with other people. Face-to-face conversation with others is very often a primary venue for the Holy Spirit to speak, move, and catalyze change.

4. Prayer and a Focus on God

   - In Acts 10, both visions that set events into motion happen during times of prayer (10:2–3, 10, 30, 11:5). Elsewhere in Acts, prayer plays an essential role in setting the stage for times of critical discernment (1:14; 4:24–31; 13:2–3; also 9:10; 16:25). In these

---

36. R. Williams, *Being Christian*, 21 (emphasis original).

instances, prayer becomes a way to focus intentionally upon God, inviting God to speak and to direct God's people.

- Today prayer is a natural starting point for discernment, as an opportunity to voice critical questions and to engage in contemplative listening. Prayer is both an individual and a communal practice, facilitating an appropriate focus upon God and God's leading.

Spiritual discernment is simply an open and intentional dialogue among constructive conversation partners, with the aim of most clearly seeing a way forward. Like in Acts, these practices of discernment strive for conclusions that a faith community may be able to affirm: "it seemed good to the Spirit and to us . . ." (Acts 15:28).

The Way of Jesus

The paths which early churches traveled, compelled by the Spirit, are not brand new. They reflect the boundary-breaking way of Jesus.

Throughout Luke's Gospel, Jesus' ministry not only engages gentiles (7:1–10; 17:11–19), but it also casts a clear vision of God's historic and ongoing interest in extending life and salvation to people outside the conventional boundaries of Israel (4:24–27; 10:25–37; 24:47; also 2:30–32). In addition to gentiles and Samaritans, Jesus intentionally engages with several other groups of people normally marginalized or decentered in Jewish society: women (8:1–3; 10:38–42; 24:11), widows (4:25–26; 7:11–17), the physically debilitated (13:10–17), tax collectors (5:30; 19:1–10), and "sinners" (5:30; 7:36–50; 15:2). In fact, Jesus' attention to marginalized peoples is a defining aspect of the salvation he brings.

For Jesus' ministry in Luke's Gospel, salvation may be at least partially described as a status reversal or a social restoration. As Justo González points out: "One of the central themes in the Gospel of Luke is what interpreters have often called 'the great reversal'—or perhaps in today's more common language we should call it 'the world upside down.'"[37] This is not just a "spiritual" change: it is a reversal that also affects realities of economics, class, honor, accessibility, privilege, authority, gender, ethnicity, and other social matters. In Luke's Gospel, the saving work of God in Jesus Christ is a reorienting force, converting and reshaping individuals and communities under the guidance of the Holy Spirit.

37. González, *Story Luke Tells*, 29.

This theme continues in the book of Acts, especially through how communities are reformed anew—with new boundaries around who may join the community of the Way. In ways that are largely envisioned in Luke's Gospel, the story of Acts makes explicit God's priority for extending the salvation of Jesus to the nations (gentiles). For this reason, some interpreters have seen "mission to the gentiles" as the pervading theme of Acts.[38] But this focus on including gentiles is not a new idea in Acts: it shows up first in the boundary-breaking, socially reorienting, radically reconfiguring ministry of Jesus.[39] The church is not called by the Holy Spirit to start something brand new: it is called simply to live out and embody the way of Jesus.

First Steps: Discernment and Engagement

A logical outcome of this chapter would be to emphasize the need to step outside our comfort zones. But chances are high such a call may not yield much change. Many Christians today are aware that God—in Scripture and in the world today—calls people outside their comfort zones. The more pressing question is: How do we know *where* to do so?

For these kinds of questions, the practices of spiritual discernment are helpful. After all, anyone can hear a general call to engage others, but unless there is clarity about focus, the call remains vague. To clarify working answers to these questions, the following subject areas and questions may be helpful. Although phrased in ways that address communities, the language may be changed to address individuals.

Questions of Spiritual Discernment

Testimonies of Experience

- What is God doing among and around us as a community? What new developments are taking shape in which God's hand may be present?
- When and where has God led us to new acts of ministry in our neighborhood and world? How are those continuing or changing?

---

38. Dupont, "Salvation of the Gentiles"; S. Wilson, *Gentiles*.

39. Of course, the theme of God's salvation being extended to the nations does not begin with Jesus' ministry but has roots throughout the writings of the Hebrew Bible. See Kaiser, *Mission in the Old Testament*; cf. Orlinsky, "Light of the Nations."

- What obstacles to ministry have happened, which may signify God's guidance or opposition?

Scripture

- In reading Scripture, what do we hear God saying? What prompts and urges arise from your reading?
- In view of God sending people to new places in Scripture, what parallels may be drawn to our contexts today?
- Scripture portrays a God who persistently calls people to be part of God's work in the world. How does this community see itself engaging in that work today?

People and Community

- What do we hear God saying through the voices of others?
- In gathering to discern, how do our voices coalesce or agree?
- How do voices within our community agree or resonate with the voices of people outside our community?

Prayer and a Focus on God

- What do we hear God saying in prayer?
- As we pray (individually and together), how do our questions or concerns change or become more refined?
- As we pray for guidance, what issues, questions, or concerns become more pressing? Which ones seem to lose significance?

Pondering these questions requires time, space, and energy. They are not engaged lightly or quickly. In fact, questions of spiritual discernment often require lengthy periods of time, to ensure adequate sitting with the questions and not settling upon easy answers. After all, clarity in discernment comes not from answers alone, but from the *process* of asking important questions.

Discernment is ongoing. It is never finished business. Even after points of clarity and arrival are found, it is not as if God stops leading. At no point in a Christian's or church's life have they arrived at a point where God's direction and activity no longer need to be discerned.

As we engage in discernment as individuals and as communities, we do so in full trust that God's Spirit is already present and active. Our call is simply to identify more precisely where that is most true.

Conclusion

In Acts, the Holy Spirit leads God's people to new places, to be with new people, and to do things they've never done before. It is no less true today.

In today's world, some of the people with whom we are called to engage may be immigrant communities, people with disabilities (physical or intellectual), single parents, the unhoused, people in socioeconomic need, people who experience hunger, people in need of mental health resources, people who have been harmed by the church, people historically marginalized by the church (like divorcees and LGBTQIA+ people), people who vote differently than us, and people who look different than us. More suggestions may be added. The people to whom God's Spirit calls you is best clarified not by others but by your faithful engagement with God's Spirit using the resources available to you.

The good news in all this is that our calling is not to invent an original and bold vision to implement, but rather to embrace what God is already up to and to get on board with it. After all, God's Holy Spirit is already active in the world. Ours is simply to discern where that is true and to say "yes" to the Spirit's prompts to get involved.

Questions for Discussion

1. This chapter suggests the story of Acts is not simply about the conversion of the nations but also about the conversion (or change in thinking) of the church. What do you think about that idea?

2. In Acts 10:1—11:18, early church leaders (like Peter) clearly struggled with a major change to conventional boundary markers for the faith community. And yet the Spirit compelled them. What parallels do you see between this scenario and the experiences of church communities and individuals today?

3. What concrete examples come to your mind of situations where church communities have faithfully (or not so faithfully) navigated traditional barriers to welcoming people?

4. This chapter concludes with emphasis on spiritual discernment, which Eugene Peterson describes as "praying with [our] eyes open."[40] How significant are practices of spiritual discernment for your faith or for your community? How could they benefit your faith and community?

5. In Acts 10:1—11:18, the Holy Spirit is active and orchestrating events around people like Peter and Cornelius. Where do you think the Holy Spirit is most active today in your life, in your church community's life, in your larger community, and in the world?

Resources for Further Exploration

- Gaventa, Beverly Roberts. *Acts.* Abingdon New Testament Commentaries. Nashville: Abingdon, 2003, pp. 162–76.
- Nouwen, Henri J. M., with Michael J. Christensen and Rebecca J. Laird. *Discernment: Reading the Signs of Daily Life.* San Francisco: HarperOne, 2013.
- Peterson, Eugene H. *The Contemplative Pastor: Returning to the Art of Spiritual Direction.* The Leadership Library 17. Carol Stream, IL: Christianity Today, 1989.
- Reed, Angela H. "Spiritual Discernment in the Congregation." *Vision* (Winnipeg) 17.1 (2016) 46–53.
- Walton, Steve. "Deciding About Deciding: Early Christian Communal Decision-Making in Acts." In *Reading Acts Theologically*, 89–106. The Library of New Testament Series 661. London: T. & T. Clark, 2022.

---

40. E. Peterson, *Contemplative Pastor*, 76–92.

Action Steps for Further Consideration

- Use Acts 10:1—11:18 as part of a discernment retreat with your faith community or with a small group. See what conclusions arise from discussion with others.

- Use the "Questions of Spiritual Discernment" near the end of the chapter with a leadership group at your faith community.

- Use the "Questions of Spiritual Discernment" near the end of the chapter with an eye to your own life and faith, perhaps in association with a spiritual retreat.

- If you do not have one already, establish a connection with a spiritual director to talk about topics and questions related to where God is leading and moving you.

- Research what ethnic and cultural groups live in your larger community. Strive to learn about the religious affiliations associated with these groups and whether there are established faith communities. Prayerfully consider ways you or your community can make connections, offering resources where helpful.

- Reach out to your neighbors whom you do not know. Strive to make friendships that are mutual, reciprocal, and enduring.

7
Sharing the Story as a Way of Life

I have told students for years that it is not their job to make the gospel relevant, as the gospel of Jesus Christ is ontologically relevant because it has to do with death and life, with meaning, with beauty. Rather than making the gospel relevant, the challenge before them as ministers of the gospel of Jesus Christ is to avoid rendering that gospel irrelevant.

—S. D. Giere[1]

IN MY LATE TEENAGE years, I wanted to do ministry in another global context.

At the time, it seemed to me like the most straightforward way to devote my life to faithful witness in a holistic way. Sure, it called for a big move and living at a distance. But the clear and concrete commitment made it attractive.

My father wasn't as warm to the idea. One day he asked: "Are you still planning to leave the country?" I said: "I think so." He said: "I think you should do what you're called to do here. Why do you need to go far away?"

I didn't have a great answer in response. In fact, I never came up with one. While open to being in a different global context, I came to realize my own distinctive calling did not require it. Like many others, I was (and am) called to faithful witness. And like for many others, that calling is not so restricted to specific geographical areas.

---

1. Giere, *Freedom and Imagination*, ix–x.

I share this story because many people associate faithful witness simply with professionals who have a special calling to that kind of thing, including those who relocate to faraway places. I once had a similar idea. I just don't think it's a helpful association.

Faithful witness is not something for professionals. Nor is it something achieved only by major moves and elaborate programs. More than anything, faithful witness is a way of life. And it is best done by everyday people wherever they are, wherever they live, with whomever they interact. While it deserves intentionality, faithful witness is less a program or strategy than it is a way of life.

In Acts, we see this play out in how early church communities lived a distinctive way of life (called "the Way"). We see it play out in how apostles like Paul bore witness wherever they were, no matter how they got there. We see it play out in how faithful witness in Acts sometimes took place in unexpected places, among unconventional people, and in unforeseen ways. In all these scenarios, early believers embraced faithful witness as a way of life.

The Unpredictable Paths of Bearing Witness

The narrative of Acts gives a lot of focus to Paul.

Starting with his reorientation or "conversion" (9:1–19a), the focus kicks more fully into gear from chapter 13 on, after the Holy Spirit sets him (and Barnabas) apart for the work to which God has called them (13:1–3). From this point on, the narrative is largely preoccupied with Paul's travels, his work nurturing new communities, his engaging with local leaders, his experiences in prison and at trial, and his journey to Rome. The sheer focus of Acts 13–28 (most of Acts) suggests there is at least something instructive and informative about Paul's ministry.[2]

What many people do not realize, however, is how unforeseen and almost arbitrary some of Paul's ministry experiences are, at least by some definitions.

First, Paul spends many years in relative obscurity before his travels begin. After his conversion experience, Paul (Saul) spends significant time in Tarsus (9:30) and Antioch (11:25–26) before being called to the work for which he is so known (13:1–3). According to Acts, Paul comes to Antioch only at Barnabas's invitation (11:25–26). Although reconciling the accounts

---

2. At 567 verses, Acts 13–28 represents 56.36 percent of Acts (Just, "New Testament Statistics").

of Acts with Galatians 1–2 yields more tensions and questions than answers, it suggests a good number of years take place after Paul's conversion before he is ready for ministry travels.³

The Conversion of St. Paul (ca. 1391–92), by Spinello Aretino, Metropolitan Museum of Art, public domain, courtesy of Wikimedia Commons

Second, Paul's journeys do not always go as planned. His first journey (13:4—14:28) encounters enough hostility to justify the comment: "It is through many persecutions that we must enter the kingdom of God"

---

3. In Galatians 1:11—2:14, Paul states that he went to Jerusalem "three years" after first spending time in Arabia and Damascus (1:17–18), and then went to "Syria and Cilicia" (1:21) which would have included Tarsus and Antioch. Acts states that Paul spent at least "an entire year" (11:25) with the church at Antioch before embarking on his mission work (13:1–3).

(14:22).⁴ In the early stages of his second journey (15:36—18:23), Paul's interest in Asia Minor is denied by the Holy Spirit, who directs him instead to Macedonia (16:6-10). On two occasions, Paul navigates a travel companion's departure (13:13; 15:37-40). At many places, hostility forces Paul out of town or elsewhere, often after very little time.⁵ Finally, while Paul's interest in seeing Rome (19:21) is fulfilled, it happens only by an arduous journey of many years in prison (19:21—28:31). Adaptive as Paul is throughout his ministry, these events are hardly ideal and expected.

Third, the responses to Paul's ministry in Acts vary widely. At most of the places where Paul begins ministry, he is forced out of town or elsewhere. On some of these occasions, he is stoned (14:19-20), threatened (21:27-36), or imprisoned (16:16-34, 21:27—28:31). By comparison, the places where Paul receives a positive response are relatively few.⁶ Although Acts is a selective account, the juxtaposition of such positive and negative responses gives the overall impression: Paul's ministry is not a story of sheer and straightforward success.

According to Acts, Paul's ministry is marked by circumstantial events, unexpected curve balls, and unfavorable responses. It depicts faithful witness, based on Paul's example, as more a series of accidental events that the Holy Spirit makes fruitful than a predictable plan. Paul's ministry in Acts is characterized far less by heroism and achievement than by trials, uncertainties, sporadic successes, and years of hard work. Hardly a sales pitch for a glamorous way of life, his ministry attests to the uncertainty and unpredictability of the work of faithful witness.

A representative example from Paul's travels is the time he spends in Athens (Acts 17:16-34). While the city setting is a historic hub of philosophical culture, Paul's activity here is more ordinary than extraordinary, and the response more mixed than miraculous. As one of just four stories

---

4. While issued as a word of encouragement to disciples in Antioch of Pisidia, its narrative placement in the journey gives Paul's comment the significance of overarching commentary. Note also how Paul's first ministry journey takes him to Cyprus and cities in south Asia Minor (13:4—14:28), to which no surviving letter of Paul's was written (save possibly Galatians). Still, Paul's evaluation is a positive one (14:27).

5. Acts 13:48-52; 14:4-7, 19-20; 16:38-40; 17:5-10, 13-14; 18:1-7, 12-18; 19:23—20:1.

6. Positive responses by numerous peoples: 13:42-43, 48-49; 17:4, 10-12; 18:8-11; 19:8-10. Positive responses by individuals or relatively few people: 13:12; 16:14-15, 32-34. Cf. 14:18, 27.

from Acts 13–28 to appear in the Revised Common Lectionary Sunday readings, it is also a story more familiar than some in Acts.[7]

Witness on the Way: Acts 17:16–34

The story begins on the heels of sudden departures. Acts recounts Paul's ministry in Philippi (16:11–40), Thessalonica (17:1–9), and Beroea (17:10–15), all of which entail crowds of people in uproar against him and his colleagues, most of which force them out of town. After the last of the three interactions, Paul's companions escort him to Athens to wait for Silas and Timothy. It is in this stage of waiting that our story happens.

> 16 While Paul was waiting for them in Athens, he was deeply distressed to see that the city was full of idols. 17 So he argued in the synagogue with the Jews and the devout persons and also in the marketplace every day with those who happened to be there. 18 Also some Epicurean and Stoic philosophers debated with him. Some said, "What does this pretentious babbler want to say?" Others said, "He seems to be a proclaimer of foreign divinities." (This was because he was telling the good news about Jesus and the resurrection.) 19 So they took him and brought him to the Areopagus and asked him, "May we know what this new teaching is that you are presenting? 20 It sounds rather strange to us, so we would like to know what it means." 21 Now all the Athenians and the foreigners living there would spend their time in nothing but telling or hearing something new.
>
> 22 Then Paul stood in front of the Areopagus and said, "Athenians, I see how extremely spiritual you are in every way. 23 For as I went through the city and looked carefully at the objects of your worship, I found among them an altar with the inscription, 'To an unknown god.' What therefore you worship as unknown, this I proclaim to you. 24 The God who made the world and everything in it, he who is Lord of heaven and earth, does not live in shrines made by human hands, 25 nor is he served by human hands, as though he needed anything, since he himself gives to all mortals life and breath and all things. 26 From one ancestor he made all peoples to inhabit the whole earth, and he allotted the times of their existence and the boundaries of the places where they would live, 27 so that they would search for God and perhaps

---

7. Acts 17:16–34 appears in Year A on the sixth Sunday of Easter. The others three texts from Acts 13–28 are 16:9–15 (Year C, sixth Sunday of Easter), 16:16–34 (Year C, seventh Sunday of Easter), and 19:1–7 (Year B, Baptism of our Lord).

fumble about for him and find him—though indeed he is not far from each one of us. 28 For 'In him we live and move and have our being'; as even some of your own poets have said,

'For we, too, are his offspring.'

29 "Since we are God's offspring, we ought not to think that the deity is like gold or silver or stone, an image formed by the art and imagination of mortals. 30 While God has overlooked the times of human ignorance, now he commands all people everywhere to repent, 31 because he has fixed a day on which he will have the world judged in righteousness by a man whom he has appointed, and of this he has given assurance to all by raising him from the dead."

32 When they heard of the resurrection of the dead, some scoffed, but others said, "We will hear you again about this." 33 At that point Paul left them. 34 But some of them joined him and became believers, including Dionysius the Areopagite and a woman named Damaris and others with them. (Acts 17:16–34)

Several features of the story show significant aspects of faithful witness.

First, the entire episode is a result of unfortunate events. On the one hand, the location (Athens) makes this story an important episode in Paul's ministry travels, since it is the historic cultural and philosophical capital of the Greco-Roman world.[8] Here Paul brings early Christianity into dialogue with Greek philosophy, pagan idolatry, and Athenian intellectual curiosity—and Luke devotes sufficient space to telling the tale. On the other hand, the only reason Paul ends up in Athens is the hostility he experiences beforehand, in three separate locations (Philippi, Thessalonica, Beroea), compelling his colleagues to get him out of town. The narrative gives no clear indication that Paul, apart from unfortunate hostilities, intended to stop here. And shortly afterward, he leaves (18:1).

This point is worth pondering: one of the most significant interactions of Paul's ministry happens in a rather unplanned way. And yet, planned or not, Paul bears witness to the message of Jesus. He does so not only because he is "deeply distressed" at the abundance of idols (17:16), but also because bearing witness is what Paul does everywhere. In that sense, his activity in

---

8. Noted by Fitzmyer, *Acts*, 600–601. Conzelmann exaggerates the story's significance as "the most momentous Christian document from the beginnings of that extraordinary confrontation between Christianity and philosophy which was destined to continue through the following centuries and to determine the entire history of the Occident" ("Address of Paul," 217). Rothschild argues the passage portrays Paul like Epimenides and a figure who facilitates the transfer of a religious movement to Athens (*Paul in Athens*).

Athens is nothing new. Whether in planned or unplanned venues, in ideal or unideal circumstances, Paul bears witness. It's just what he does. And in doing so, happenstance situations became significant.[9]

Second, Paul's witness keys into contextual realities and responds to them. Even though Paul proclaims about Jesus in many various settings, he does so here in a way that attunes distinctively to his audience. His speech at the Areopagus, for example, is at the invitation of local people engaged in philosophy (17:19-20). Even more distinctive is how Paul's message uses language intended to resonate with their experience: different from earlier speeches in Acts, this one does not allude to Israel's history, does not quote Scripture, and refers to Jesus only indirectly as "a man whom [God] has appointed, . . . raising him from the dead" (17:31).[10] These contrasts are so noticeable that some interpreters have wondered if the speech is a foreign insertion in Acts.[11] However, the speech's theology and message are consistent with speeches throughout Acts, just with stronger emphasis on the universal scope of God's jurisdiction.[12] These traits make the speech not an intrusion but a translation of a message consistent throughout Acts into language familiar to the contextual audience.[13]

Translation is a fitting descriptor for Paul's witness here, since his activity clearly strives to build bridges. Not only does his speech take place at the invitation of Epicureans and Stoic philosophers (v. 18), but both his concerns and speech resonate with principles and concerns of Stoicism and Epicureanism in his day.[14] Paul's speech affirms their religious devotion

---

9. For another good example of Paul bearing witness in contextual ways in unexpected circumstances, see his acts of hospitality and grace on the sea journey to Rome (Acts 27:1—28:15, esp. 27:21-26, 33-38; 28:8-10).

10. Cf. earlier speeches in Acts for allusions to Israel's history (2:29, 7:2-47, 13:17-25), quotations from Scripture (2:17-21, 25-28; 3:22-23; 4:11; 13:33), and more explicit naming of Jesus (2:32; 3:15; 4:10; 13:30, 37).

11. Dibelius, "Paul on the Areopagus." Dibelius suggests "the theology of the Areopagus speech is absolutely foreign to Paul's own theology, . . . it is, in fact, foreign to the entire New Testament" (71).

12. For example, see "offspring" language in 3:25, God as Creator in 4:24-30, God not dwelling in "buildings made by human hands" in 7:48, and calls to repentance throughout speeches in Acts (2:39; 3:21; 10:34; 14:15-17). See Schubert, "Place of the Areopagus Speech"; Gärtner, *Areopagus Speech*. As a speech emphasizing the universal sovereignty of the God who raised Jesus from the dead, calling all people in response to repent, its overarching themes correspond with earlier speeches in Acts.

13. Gaventa, *Acts*, 247.

14. The connections with Stoicism are strong: the Stoic emphasis on the unity of

(v. 22), takes cues from local inscriptions (v. 23), and begins with reasoning from creation that may readily be appreciated by philosophically minded Athenians (vv. 24–26). Paul goes on to quote two Greek philosopher-poets, Epimenides and Aratus, to make the points: God "is not far from each one of us" and "we are God's offspring" (vv. 27–29).[15] In view of these realities, Paul invites hearers to relinquish idolatry (v. 29), to repent (v. 30), and—it is implied—to direct their devotion to the God who raised Jesus from the dead (v. 31). As Beverly Roberts Gaventa points out, Paul's speech takes "basic presuppositions of the Christian gospel and translate[s] them into language available to the narrative audience."[16]

Third, Paul's speech gets a mixed response. Some scoff; others want to hear more; and a few respond favorably (vv. 32–34). The spectrum of responses is wide. More to the point, Luke's language characterizes the response as divided. He uses a grammatical construction often used to hold contrasting ideas in tension: "some (*hoi men* . . .) scoffed, but others (*hoi de*) said . . ." (v. 32). Only the ending of Acts uses the same language (*hoi men* . . . , *hoi de* . . .) to portray a response similarly divided at Paul's message (28:24–25a).[17] Although it is possible to hear the statement in 17:32 ("We will hear you again about this") as a polite dismissal, it is set in contrast with scoffers and it allows for the limited positive response at the end (v. 34).[18] Right after the divided response, Luke concludes: "At that point Paul left them" (v. 33).[19] Almost in passing, Luke adds that "some" became believers:

---

humanity (17:26), divine oversight of seasons and natural boundaries (v. 26), the divine environment in which human beings live and move (v. 26), and humanity's natural kinship with God (v. 28). That Paul takes issue with Athenian devotion to many unknown idols (17:16, 23) resonates with Epicurean resistance against religious superstition. C. K. Barrett, "Paul's Speech," 72–75.

15. The quotations are from the sixth century BCE Cretan philosopher and poet Epimenides (Acts 17:28a) and from the third century BCE poet Aratus (*Phaenomena* 5) (Acts 17:28b).

16. Gaventa, *Acts*, 254. See also Gaventa, "Traditions in Conversation."

17. The verb "scoffed" (*echleuazon*) also echoes the initial mixed response to multiple languages being spoken at Pentecost, where all were amazed and perplexed, but some "others" scoffed (*diachleuazontes*) (2:12–13). Acts 2:13 and 17:32 are the only New Testament occurrences of these verbal forms (*chleuazō, diachleuazō*).

18. So also C. K. Barrett, "Paul's Speech," 71.

19. C. K. Barrett sees the phrase *ek mesou autōn* in "left them" (lit. left "from their midst") as suggesting a hostile reaction (cf. Luke 4:30; Acts 23:10). But the phrase "from their midst" is insufficient grounds upon which to judge an entire scene's characterization, as Barrett himself admits: "The evidence is hardly adequate for us to describe the expression as a Lucan formula for escape from danger" ("Paul's Speech," 71).

Dionysius, Damaris, and "others with them" (v. 34). The observation is tacked on more like an afterthought to the scene than a closing emphasis.[20]

The response to Paul's ministry in Athens is markedly indecisive. While reactions vary throughout Acts—from warm reception to hostile rejection—this is one of the most indecisive of all.[21] We know nothing more and hear nothing further about the few who respond favorably. We have no clear indications that a church community started in Athens. Joseph Fitzmyer labels the result "little success in Athens."[22] The narrative continues simply: "After this Paul left Athens" (18:1). As far as we know, Paul never returns to the city.

Witness on the Way: Reflections for Today

Paul's example in Athens suggests several things about faithful witness.

First, it happens where we are—not where we wish to be, where we intend to be, or where we "ought" to be. By most readings of Acts, Paul ends up in Athens due to unforeseen circumstances. Whatever the cause of his arrival, he tends to the work of witness where he is. The same is true of ourselves. Faithful witness to the gospel in word and deed does not require designated spaces or intentional times. It happens anywhere and everywhere, whether we intend it or not. In fact, the ways in which we live out our faith precisely when witness is not at the forefront of our minds are often when it becomes most authentic and evident.

A friend of mine told me a story about a woman who joined his church. When asked what prompted this, she shared that she worked at a restaurant in town where people from many churches came for Sunday lunch. Among them all, "people from this church always treated me with respect—and tipped the best." She was interested in a church that practiced what they preached, especially with waitstaff at restaurants. For her, those

---

20. C. Williams characterizes this verse as showing "a lack of finish out of keeping with the rest of the chapter" (*Acts*, 207).

21. Cf. 28:24–25 for another mixed response. All other reactions are more decisive, from outright rejection (13:45–51; 18:6; also 22:1–24) to warm reception (16:11–15), or a mixture of both warm reception by some *and* outright hostility by others (13:6–12; 14:11–20; 17:4–10, 11–14; 19:9–12, 23–41).

22. Fitzmyer, *Acts*, 603. Fitzmyer partially attributes this to Paul's speech being "interrupted," but Haenchen rightly points out this is no reason to view the speech as somehow "a fragment requiring to be supplemented" (*Acts*, 526; also Dibelius, "Paul on the Areopagus," 77).

acts of consistent kindness became a witness to the gospel that was authentically lived out.

Second, faithful witness responds to the needs and issues around. In Acts 17, Paul engages in witness by responding to the things around him: signs of religious devotion, an air of philosophical inquiry, and an invitation from locals to speak further. At this invitation, more than some occasions in Acts, Paul does not launch into a scripted message with stock language. Instead, he speaks intentionally to this context, asking questions about local religious devotion, quoting philosophical voices that may have been familiar, and speaking about Jesus in language, terms, and thinking that might be more readily understood and embraced by his audience.

This approach is instructive to witness today. Faithful witness is less about stock messages and programs than it is organic engagement with local people and their needs and concerns. In contexts like twenty-first-century America, people do not lack resources to hear and learn about the Christian faith. What many do lack are people of faith who take time to befriend others, strive to know their concerns, and can think about the gospel as a message of love and liberation in relation to daily life today. As Paul's example in Acts 17 shows, this may require nontraditional lingo and a different approach. It may be challenging and may take time. But the opportunities for mutual listening and learning are worth it.

Third, bearing witness yields unpredictable results. In Athens, Paul's extensive speech gets a very indecisive response. In fact, a wide variety of responses happen, from scoffing to receptivity to wanting to hear more. It's a far cry from the response at Pentecost. This goes to show: faithful witness is not guaranteed warm reception. Certainly, this is the case with Paul's ministry in Acts. It is also true today. However faithful, conscientious, sensitive, and attentive witness may be, the response is outside our control.

As Paul experiences at Athens, faithful witness very often results in mixed responses, from apathy to openness, from dismissiveness to interest. After all, acts of faithful witness are ideally not isolated events but part of an array of experiences that build bridges and relationships. The goal is to open doors (vs. shut them), to begin conversations (vs. close them), and to invite people to hear and learn more about the story. If that is all that is accomplished, it will be enough.

In an article titled "Reading Luke-Acts from Back to Front," Loveday Alexander reads Luke and Acts as a two-volume narrative. She notes that, whereas Luke's Gospel begins with stories of prophetic pronouncements and visits from angels, the later chapters of Acts, in contrast, "negotiate the voyage back to the everyday world where the rest of us live, a world where prophets and angels have receded back into a mythical past, but where the more mundane and open-ended tasks of teaching and persuasion continue 'unhindered.'"[23] Although these words refer more to later chapters of Acts than Paul in Athens per se, they capture the "everyday" nature of witness in texts as these: without angelic interventions, without dramatic responses, and without clear markers of "success." As Paul's example increasingly shows in the later chapters of Acts, faithful witness takes place in many and various places, often mundane but nonetheless important, in response to specific situations and people, with no promises of warm reception. In such settings, faithful witness persists, leaving the results in God's hands.

First Steps: Faithful Witness Where We Are

As stated earlier, faithful witness happens where we are—not where we wish to be, where we intend to be, or where we think we "ought" to be. The best starting place is right where we already are. Given that, we might begin by simply taking notice of the people, practical realities, and opportunities around us. We might begin by simply asking questions that prompt us to look around and take notice:

- Who are the people with whom I interact regularly?
- What are the challenges and needs faced by my neighbors, my community members, and the people around me?
- How can I listen more intentionally to the people in my community and their experiences?
- What signs of spirituality and faith are present in the contexts and people around me? How might I learn more about these things?
- Where are there ready connections between the gospel and the needs, interests, desires, and experiences of those around me?

Faithful witness often does not require relocating. There are ample opportunities right where we are.

That said, faithful witness may lead us to new places. In Acts 17, Paul is in a new city. Whatever the circumstances that brought him there, he

---

23. Alexander, "Reading Luke-Acts," 446.

finds it a unique opportunity for engaging others with the story of Jesus. Intentional, constructive witness may compel us to enter new relationships and spaces more thoughtfully than we have done in the past. It may involve forging new relationships. It may involve time in a new area of our community. It may involve volunteering at a new ministry or place of service. In short, it may involve stepping outside our comfort zones to try something new. To that end, we may ponder some of the following questions:

- Who are the people in my community with whom I do not interact regularly—but might?
- How might I be more intentional about building relationships with people in my surrounding community?
- What are the real areas of need in my community? Who are the people who experience these? How may I learn about them and their experiences more intentionally?
- Where are there ready connections between the gospel and the needs, interests, desires, and experiences of those who live in areas of my community where I don't often go?

As seen in Acts, the first followers of Jesus were called to be witnesses to "the end of the earth" (1:8). That required entering new spaces. This call still stands for us today, even though it may take shape in different ways in our lives.

Responding to the Needs Around Us

On the Areopagus, Paul begins his speech this way: "Athenians, I see how extremely spiritual you are in every way" (Acts 17:22). These words are not far from the mark when it comes to describing the world in which we live today.

Countless studies have pointed out how in the United States of America the sharpest growth in religious affiliation in recent decades is in an amorphous group called the "unaffiliated." These are individuals with no specific religious association or affiliation. Some were once church people but are no longer. Others did not grow up with any religious affiliation. Still others are quite spiritual or religious in practice, but they prefer not to be affiliated with a particular movement. Although recent surveys point out that the growth of this group has tapered or even leveled off recently, estimates still suggest that the unaffiliated now make up nearly 30 percent of the US population—and about 40 percent of US people under thirty years old.[24]

Most distinctive of all is that many of the "unaffiliated" profess to be spiritual. Many of them are neither atheists nor hostile toward faith and spirituality. They simply have not yet found compelling reasons to join established communities of faith.[25] In the words of a neighbor of mine: "I believe in God. I just don't do church."

These realities suggest, certainly in the United States, that there is significant openness to Christian spirituality, faith, and witness. Many of those unaffiliated with religious communities are interested in spirituality, appreciative of positive examples of faith, and desiring to be ethical contributors to a greater good. They just don't yet see the significance of participating in the Christian way.[26]

There is a significant opportunity here for faithful witness. Many people in US society today are, like those in Athens, "extremely spiritual . . . in every way." They just don't have an explicit faith profession or a connection to a faith community. Although some have negative experiences and associations with church communities, most are not hostile to the way of Jesus. In fact, they welcome a witness that honors their experience, affirms their dignity, and conveys the message of Jesus in language that makes sense to them. Faithful witness simply needs to tap into the interests, questions, and desires of those who live around us.

It begins first with listening to those around us, their experiences, and their concerns. That takes time and energy. Eugene Peterson has pointed out:

> Listening is in short supply in the world today; people aren't used to being listened to. . . . Speaking to people does not have the same personal intensity as listening to them. The question I put to myself is not "How many people have you spoken to about Christ this week?" but "How many people have you listened to in Christ this week?"[27]

---

24. G. Smith, "Religiously Unaffiliated"; Public Religion Research, "PRRI 2021 Census"; P. Smith, "America's Nonreligious"; Pew Research, "Religious 'Nones.'" On the recent tapering of this group's growth, see G. Smith and Cooperman, "Rise of Religious 'Nones.'"

25. P. Smith, "America's Nonreligious."

26. P. Smith, "America's Nonreligious."

27. E. Peterson, *Contemplative Pastor*, 30–31.

When it comes to engaging the people around us, it begins with listening. To listen to our neighbors is to show them authentic care and love. To listen is an act of love. To begin with listening is to lead with love.

In listening, we learn how to respond. And responding faithfully involves responding in ways and words that people can understand. As Paul's example in Acts 17 suggests, faithful witness in familiar and new spaces calls for speaking about the faith in new language, different than what we may be used to. However mixed the results may be, a constructive and positive witness will not be in vain.

Conclusions: The Way of Witness and the Way of Jesus

In an interview conversation, Eugene Peterson captures the call to faithful witness well:

> The whole task of the Christian witness is to do what Jesus did—is to incarnate the presence of God, the action of God, the words of God, wherever you are. And one of the remarkable things about Jesus' life is . . . he was comfortable in the temple, comfortable in synagogues, but he didn't spend most of his time there. Most of this time was in the marketplace, fields, around people's tables, on the streets.[28]

As Peterson notes, faithful witness does not simply mean being an envoy of a particular message. The call to faithful witness is a holistic call to live more fully into the way of Jesus—his life, his ministry, and his radical hospitality. This makes the call to bear witness—in both new and old spaces, in both new and familiar language—nothing other than the call to follow Jesus, to live as he did, and to love as he loved.

Some people have negative associations with "evangelism" language. Far fewer have negative associations with Jesus and what he stood for. The call to faithful witness, at the end of the day, is simply a calling to embody the presence and way of Jesus in the world, in our dealings with others, and in our daily lives. This makes the call to faithful witness inseparable from the call of Jesus: "follow me."

---

28. E. Peterson, "What Faith Looks Like." Peterson continues: "And he wasn't less religious or less sacred when he was having dinner with the Pharisees, with the prostitutes, with the tax collectors, than he was in the temple and in the synagogue."

Sharing the Story as a Way of Life

Questions for Discussion

1. This chapter portrays Paul's ministry as more characterized by unpredictability and unforeseen events than playing out as he may have expected. How does this make you think about Paul's ministry and work?

2. Have a look at Acts 17:16–34. This chapter has portrayed Paul as responding attentively in Athens to the context in which he finds himself. How do you see this to be true? Are there ways you think Paul could have responded more faithfully?

3. Faithful witness starts best with where we are—in our homes, neighborhoods, communities, and existing relationships. What opportunities do you see in these places for faithful witness? Consider the first list of questions under the section "First Steps" to ponder further.

4. Faithful witness may invite us into new spaces, outside our comfort zones. Where might this be for you? Consider the second list of questions under the section "First Steps" to ponder further.

5. This chapter suggests that the spirituality of "unaffiliated" people offers a significant opportunity for faithful witness today. Do you agree? Why or why not?

6. At the end of this chapter, the call to faithful witness is described as inseparable from the call to follow Jesus. How does this sit with you?

Resources for Further Exploration

- Acts 13–28 (mostly Paul's ministry travels). Notice especially the events that are neither successful nor ideal. Where is God present and leading in these events?
- Gaventa, Beverly Roberts. "Traditions in Conversation and Collision: Reflections on Multiculturalism in the Acts of the Apostles." In *Making Room at the Table: An Invitation to Multicultural Worship*, edited by Brian K. Blount and Leonora Tubbs Tisdale, 30–41. Louisville: Westminster John Knox, 2001.
- Giere, S. D. *Freedom and Imagination: Trusting Christ in an Age of Bad Faith*. Minneapolis: Fortress, 2023.

- Resources about the religiously unaffiliated:

    a. Public Religion Research Institute Staff. "PRRI 2021 Census of American Religion, Updates and Trends." April 27, 2022. https://www.prri.org/spotlight/prri-2021-american-values-atlas-religious-affiliation-updates-and-trends-white-christian-decline-slows-unaffiliated-growth-levels-off/.

    b. Pew Research Center. "Religious 'Nones' in America: Who They Are and What They Believe." January 24, 2024. https://pewrsr.ch/3SedVTm.

    c. Smith, Peter. "America's Nonreligious Are a Growing, Diverse Phenomenon. They Really Don't Like Organized Religion." Associated Press News, October 4, 2023. https://apnews.com/article/nonreligious-united-states-nones-spirituality-humanist-91bb8430280c88fd88530a7ad64b03f8.

- Schertz, Mary H. "'This Was Not Done in a Corner': Lessons on Proclamation from the Book of Acts." *Vision* (Winnipeg) 18.2 (Fall 2017) 86–93.

Action Steps for Further Consideration

- Do some research on trends and traits of the religiously unaffiliated in US society, starting with some of the suggested resources above. What did you learn? How does this make you think differently about the call to faithful witness in the years to come?

- Ask someone you know, with whom you have an established relationship, who identifies as nonreligious or unaffiliated what some of their views are about faith and spirituality. If comfortable, ask what might interest them (if anything) in a religious tradition or faith community. Listen carefully and learn.

- This chapter shared an example of a woman who joined a church especially because its people were kind and generous at her workplace. Consider ways that you (or your church community) may be setting a similar example—or a negative one.

- Volunteer at a shelter, a feeding ministry, or another place of social service in a part of your community where you do not regularly go. While serving, listen and learn.

- Compose a paragraph (or page or two) responding to the question "Why I am a Christian." Strive to use language you think would be understandable to someone without any church background. Be open to using some of this language, if called for, in conversation with others.

Conclusion
A Word of Promise

> In a society where we are surrounded by people of various religious and non-religious traditions—and where there is a frequent distortion of who Jesus was, is, and will be for us—it is the right time for Christians to reclaim how we define and confess the Gospel.
>
> —SARA FUNKHOUSER[1]

THE WORLD IS A rapidly changing place. That is not just a subjective feeling. Although many things remain constant, several studies suggest more dramatic changes have happened in recent decades, especially in industrialized societies like the United States.[2] For example, life expectancy rates have increased significantly; most people travel for leisure; some healthcare resources are more readily accessible; advanced degrees in education are more common; religious affiliations have shifted significantly; the internet is considered a necessity of life; and social media is becoming a primary means by which people hear news, typically through their phones. While there are all kinds of exceptions to these generalizations, they are enough to show: significant changes have happened in recent decades, at least in some parts of the world.

In a rapidly changing world, it is more challenging to identify what faithful witness looks like. Not terribly long ago, there were mainstream

---

1. Funkhouser, "Freed to Proclaim" 38.

2. See, for example, Kozek, *Globe Is Changing*; Engelhart, *How the World Has Changed*; Cohn and Caumont, "10 Demographic Trends"; Abadi, "11 Dramatic Ways"; Zerzan, "How Has the World Changed."

CONCLUSION

approaches to evangelism (whether or not they were helpful). Today, for good reasons, what faithful witness entails is less clear.

Here is the good news: we are not the first followers of the Way to navigate uncharted territory. We are not the first followers of Jesus to live in a pluralistic society with a range of reactions toward our faith. We come from a long line of faithful followers, who have lived out their witness in various ways. Even when their efforts have not been successful, the God of Jesus Christ has been faithful.

A story that illustrates some of these realities is the ending of Acts, especially the final scene. As part of this book's conclusion, it is only fitting to consider the conclusion of Acts.

The Ending of Acts (28:16–31): A Word of Promise

> 16 When we came into Rome, Paul was allowed to live by himself, with the soldier who was guarding him.
> 17 Three days later he called together the local leaders of the Jews. When they had assembled, he said to them, "Brothers, though I had done nothing against our people or the customs of our ancestors, yet I was arrested in Jerusalem and handed over to the Romans. 18 When they had examined me, the Romans wanted to release me because there was no reason for the death penalty in my case. 19 But when the Jews objected, I was compelled to appeal to the emperor—even though I had no charge to bring against my people. 20 For this reason therefore I asked to see you and speak with you, since it is for the sake of the hope of Israel that I am bound with this chain." 21 They replied, "We have received no letters from Judea about you, and none of the brothers coming here has reported or spoken anything evil about you. 22 But we would like to hear from you what you think, for with regard to this sect we know that everywhere it is spoken against."
> 23 After they had set a day to meet with him, they came to him at his lodgings in great numbers. From morning until evening he explained the matter to them, testifying to the kingdom of God and trying to convince them about Jesus both from the law of Moses and from the prophets. 24 Some were convinced by what he had said, while others refused to believe. 25 So they disagreed with each other, and as they were leaving Paul made one further statement: "The Holy Spirit was right in saying to your ancestors through the prophet Isaiah, 26 'Go to this people and say, You will

> indeed listen but never understand, and you will indeed look but never perceive. 27 For this people's heart has grown dull, and their ears are hard of hearing, and they have shut their eyes; otherwise they might look with their eyes and listen with their ears and understand with their heart and turn—and I would heal them.' 28 "Let it be known to you, then, that this salvation of God has been sent to the gentiles; they will listen."
>
> 30 He lived there two whole years at his own expense and welcomed all who came to him, 31 proclaiming the kingdom of God and teaching about the Lord Jesus Christ with all boldness and without hindrance. (Acts 28:16–31)

The ending of Acts has fascinated people for millennia.

By most standards, both ancient and modern, it ends abruptly. Paul has arrived at Rome (28:16), which has long been foreshadowed (19:21). Some readers believe this fulfills the promise of witness "to the end of the earth" (1:8), but witness arrived here long before Paul (28:14–15). Plus, most ancient sources call Rome the world's center, not its end. More importantly, Paul does not stand trial before Caesar as expected (23:11; 27:23–25). Most of all, the ending does not make Paul's fate clear. Although earlier omens and the time frame of "two years" (28:30) suggest some things, the ending never truly says what happens to Paul. While some interpreters suggest ancient readers "knew" what happened, surviving sources from antiquity show no signs of an unspoken shared understanding.[3]

Interpreters have speculated many things about why the ending concludes as it does: Luke did not know what came next, or did not want to narrate it, or died before finishing the book, or intended another volume (unfinished or lost), for example. Although probing Luke's intentions is intriguing, his intentions are lost to history. All that can be truly said is not *why* Acts ends this way, but *that* it does.

Adding to the ending's open-ended nature is the last interaction. Paul's dialogue with the Jewish religious leaders in Rome is very inconclusive: "Some were convinced . . . , while others refused to believe. So they disagreed with each other" (vv. 24–25a). While some readers believe the Isaiah quotation is a conclusive judgment about unreceptive hearers, immediately afterward Paul welcomes "all" (v. 30), implying no conclusive judgment has been rendered. The quotation functions like a prophetic rebuke, in the tradition of Israel's prophets, more than a definitive

---

3. For fuller discussion of aspects and theories about the ending, see Troftgruben, *Conclusion Unhindered*, 7–36 and 144–78.

Conclusion

judgment. At the close, the ending of Acts leaves off with more irresolution than decisive judgment.

But the narrative ends with more than simply ambiguity and mixed reactions. It ends with witness to the gospel continuing in full force:

> 30 He lived there two whole years at his own expense and welcomed all who came to him, 31 proclaiming the kingdom of God and teaching about the Lord Jesus Christ with all boldness and without hindrance. (Acts 28:30–31)

Some readers see these closing lines as primarily about Paul's legacy—a final portrait of him doing what he does best. This reading portrays Paul as quite the apostle, setting a high standard for others to attain. Personally, I think this reading puts emphasis on the wrong syllable. The closing scene of Acts is less focused upon Paul per se than on what he is *doing*: bearing witness in an ongoing way, no matter the obstacles and hindrances. With this emphasis, the closing scene more readily invites readers to join and play the game themselves.

First, in the closing scene (28:30–31) Paul is not named. He is merely assumed from the preceding passage. The only ones explicitly named are those central to Paul's message: God, the Lord Jesus Christ, and—by allusion ("boldness")—the Holy Spirit (v. 31).[4] In this way, the closing scene emphasizes the central actors of Paul's story more than the apostle himself.

Second, the closing scene is representative of witness throughout the narrative. Paul uses resources responsibly, welcomes all who will listen, proclaims the kingdom of God, teaches about Jesus, and is empowered by a Spirit-inspired boldness (28:30–31).[5] This makes the scene representative of witness throughout Acts, not just Paul's ministry.

Third, earlier on, in his last extended speech in Acts, Paul characterizes his ministry as entirely at Jesus' initiative (26:16–18). More to the point, Paul depicts his witness as about a Messiah who himself is actually the proclaimer:

---

4. Throughout Acts, "boldness" of speech is an activity inspired by the Spirit: 4:13, 29, 31; 9:27–28; 13:46; 14:3; 18:26; 19:8; 26:26; 28:31.

5. On the responsible use of resources: Acts 1:18; 2:43–45; 4:32–37; 5:1–11, 12–16; 16:16–18; 18:3; 19:24–27; 20:33–34. On proclaiming the kingdom of God: 1:3; 8:12; 19:8. On teaching about Jesus: 4:2, 18; 5:21, 42; 11:26; 13:1; 15:35; 17:19; 18:11, 25; 20:20. On being empowered by a boldness inspired by the Spirit: 4:13, 29, 31; 9:27–28; 13:46; 14:3; 18:26; 19:8; 26:26. That Paul proclaims "the kingdom of God" also connects his witness to the message proclaimed by Jesus in Luke's Gospel (Luke 4:43; 8:1, 10; Acts 1:3).

> 22 To this day I have had help from God, and so I stand here, testifying to both small and great, saying nothing but what the prophets and Moses said would take place: 23 that the Messiah must suffer and that, by being the first to rise from the dead, he would proclaim light both to our people and to the gentiles. (Acts 26:22–23)

Here the proclaimed has become the proclaimer.[6] Paul's final speech is a climactic summary of his witness throughout Acts.[7] As such, it influences how we read the closing scene: less as a portrayal of Paul the valorous apostle, and more about witness as an act at *Jesus'* initiative.

Finally, the closing words of Acts 28:30–31—"with all boldness [*parrēsia*] and without hindrance [*akōlutōs*]"—suggest the enduring nature of this witness is due less to Paul's persistence than to divine agency. Throughout Acts, "boldness" is a gift of the Spirit.[8] Further, the language of "hindrance" (*kōluō*) in Luke-Acts often refers to human resistance to God's designs.[9] Peter, for example, concludes his retelling of events associated with Cornelius: "who was I that I would be able to hinder [*kōlusai*] God?" (11:17). The fact that witness continues "unhindered" at the end suggests no resistance, human or otherwise, will be able to hinder the enduring work of Spirit-empowered witness. These closing emphases draw attention to the agency and initiative of God underneath Paul's witness.[10]

Why does this matter? It changes how we read and hear the closing scene of Acts.

If the scene is primarily about Paul and how great an apostle he was, then the story reads like a heroic example we are called to emulate: "Be like Paul."

---

6. Noted by Gaventa, *Acts*, 348. In this final speech, Paul claims for himself only that he persecuted the saints (26:10–11). See also O'Toole, *Christological Climax*, 76–78.

7. Robert Tannehill calls it "a climactic summary of Paul's mission as the narrator wants it to be remembered" (*Narrative Unity*, 2:329).

8. See 4:13, 29, 31; 9:27–28; 13:46; 14:3; 18:26; 19:8; 26:26; 28:31; Van Unnik, "Christian's Freedom of Speech," 477–82. In fact, the full phrase "with all boldness" appears elsewhere only in 4:29–31, when the apostles first pray to speak with boldness—and receive the Spirit's empowerment in response.

9. See Luke 9:49–50; 11:52; 18:16; Acts 10:47; 11:17; also 8:36. Other uses of *kōluō* are Luke 6:29; 23:2; Acts 16:6; 24:23; 27:43. In Acts 16:6, the word refers to the Holy Spirit's "hindering" of Paul and his companions from speaking the word in Asia. See Mealand, "Close of Acts."

10. Some of the points made in this section are also highlighted in different ways in Troftgruben, *Conclusion Unhindered*, 166–68, 172–73.

Conclusion

But the scene's rhetorical point is not simply to be like Paul—it is to bear witness like Paul did. And it is not because Paul was so great. It is because God in Christ by the power of the Holy Spirit enables people like Paul to bear witness "with all boldness and without hindrance."

The closing scene of Acts reads less like a straightforward call to action or emulation than it does a word of promise about faithful witness as something empowered and enabled by God. In this sense, the ending is not simply a call to "go do": it's an invitation to join a movement already in motion. The work of witness is finally the work of God, about a message about Christ, empowered by the Spirit of God.

Maybe I am splitting hairs about the closing scene of Acts and how it is read. But I think this matters. It suggests the book does not end with a simple command "Do this." It ends with a more nuanced message "*God is doing this*," with the implication: "Will you join the movement?" In Lutheran theological terms, it changes the closing scene from a reading that is primarily law (demand) to a reading that is primarily gospel (promise).[11]

The Work of Ongoing Witness Today

The closing scene of Acts, I think, reads like a word of promise for the church today.

Church communities today face many complicated challenges, certainly in places like the United States. Trust in institutionalized Christianity is low. Religious apathy is on the rise. Skepticism about religious leaders and critiques of church communities have grown. Financial support for church ministries is shifting. Political polarization is steeply growing. Church denominational structures are undergoing major changes. In short, there is more change afoot than stability for many church communities in the Western world.

Apart from church, impressions of the Christian faith in general are also challenged. A 2020 Barna study, for example, shows that most non-Christians in the United States today (52 percent) have an unfavorable

---

11. This distinction is a theological one, not a biblical one. Martin Luther read the whole of Scripture through the lens of law and gospel, not just certain portions. While this distinction does not help foster a nuanced view of "law" in Scripture, it is a useful one for thinking theologically about divine vs. human activity in reading Scripture. See, for example, "Freedom of a Christian," *LW* 31:348; Apology 4, *Book of Concord* 121; Smalcald Articles 3.2-4, *Book of Concord* 311-19.

impression of Christianity as a religious faith.[12] The very same percentage also believes the Christian church is no longer relevant in today's world.[13] In increasing ways, constructive witness in a society with baggage around Christianity is like a walk uphill against the wind.

However, the narrative of Acts reminds us: God, Jesus, and the Spirit call, inspire, empower, and enable faithful witness in the world—in spite of obstacles, in spite of cold reception, no matter the circumstances. Just as early witnesses in Acts were empowered to bear witness with boldness and without hindrance, so are followers of Jesus today empowered by the Holy Spirit to do the same. In short, followers of Jesus have navigated uncharted waters before. And the God of Jesus Christ, by the power of the Holy Spirit, has not left them hanging.

As followers of Jesus today, we are not faced with obstacles and uncertainty more daunting than faced by past witnesses. In their day and ours, God has empowered, emboldened, and enabled faithful witness. This God will not fail to continue to assist us with faithful witness today and in the years to come, however uncertain our paths are.

The call to faithful witness is an invitation and a movement for us to join, whatever our abilities and frailties. The story of Acts, after all, is a story about God at work in the world through the Holy Spirit, with followers and witnesses of Jesus just trying to keep up. That's a story in which we have a part, whose ultimate conclusion is yet to be written.

Conclusion: Witness as a Way of Life

In a 2023 *Atlantic* article, Jake Meador makes an observation about American society in the twenty-first century:

> Contemporary America simply isn't set up to promote mutuality, care, or common life. Rather, it is designed to maximize individual accomplishment as defined by professional and financial success.... Workism reigns in America, and because of it, community in America, religious community included, is a math problem that doesn't add up.[14]

---

12. With 21 percent responding "very unfavorable" and 31 percent "somewhat unfavorable." Barna, "Five Trends."

13. With 24 percent responding "definitely agree" and 28 percent "somewhat agree." Barna, "Five Trends."

14. Meador, "Misunderstood Reason."

Conclusion

He suggests many churches have gotten caught up in this culture of productivity and programmatic success, focusing on performance instead of being "a community that through its preaching and living bears witness to another way to live."[15]

What Christian communities are called to today is to bear witness to an alternative way of life, patterned after the way of Jesus, centered in the transforming power of the gospel. Many who identify as nonreligious (or religiously unaffiliated) do not believe they want or need a community to offer practical life tips, superb programming, or a warm welcome. While nice things, churches are hardly the only communities offering them. More distinctive is a community who lives and proclaims an alternative way of life, forgiven and set free by the message of Jesus, affirmed as God's beloved, and empowered by the Spirit to make a difference. What is most needed is a community who lives, believes, and shares the Way of Jesus in word and deed—in creative, diverse, and contextual ways.

In this book's introduction, I discuss the language of "evangelical" and its associations in twenty-first-century American society. Whether we embrace such language or not, the call to be a people invested in sharing the good news of Jesus today remains. The call of Jesus to faithful witness still stands. We just find that responding to the call faithfully today requires increased sensitivity, thoughtfulness, and integrity.

Followers of Jesus are called to bear witness to an alternative way of life. This witness involves personal testimony, a message conveyed in word and deed, conveyed in public and in private conversation, and shared in new spaces and in new ways. We will often not get it right. And the responses will vary widely. But the God who through Jesus Christ has invited us to be witnesses will be faithful through, in spite of, and all around our efforts.

Questions for Discussion

1. After reading this book, what do you think about the language "bearing witness"?
2. What comes to your mind when you think of challenges faced today by the church, the Christian faith, and faithful witness in the world today?

---

15. Meador, "Misunderstood Reason."

3. Consider Acts 28:30–31. How does this chapter's proposed reading—as a word of promise—make you hear the ending of Acts differently?

4. What examples come to your mind when you think of faithful witness by the church in today's world?

5. Reread the final paragraph of the conclusion (above). How does this book move you to think, act, or live differently in response to Jesus' call to faithful witness today?

Resources for Further Exploration

- Funkhouser, Sara A. "Freed to Proclaim: Evangelism and Discipleship." *Currents in Theology and Mission* 49.2 (April 2022) 38–41. https://currentsjournal.org/index.php/currents/article/view/349.

- Meador, Jake. "The Misunderstood Reason Millions of Americans Stopped Going to Church." *Atlantic*, July 2023. https://www.theatlantic.com/ideas/archive/2023/07/christian-church-communitiy-participation-drop/674843/.

- Nessan, Craig L. "After the Death of Evangelism—The Resurrection of an Evangelizing Church." In *The Evangelizing Church: A Lutheran Contribution*, edited by Richard H. Bliese and Craig Van Gelder, 113–32. Minneapolis: Augsburg Fortress, 2005.

- Peterson, Cheryl M. *Who Is the Church? An Ecclesiology for the Twenty-First Century.* Minneapolis: Fortress, 2013.

- Troftgruben, Troy M. *A Conclusion Unhindered: A Study of the Ending of Acts Within Its Literary Environment.* Tübingen: Mohr Siebeck, 2010, esp. 144–78 (ch. 5).

Action Steps for Further Consideration

- Identify your top reasons why someone might join your Christian community. If you have a nonreligious friend who would be comfortable hearing, share these with them and invite your friend's reflections. Learn from what your friend offers.

Conclusion

- Discuss with someone else the impressions that come to your mind when you think of the word "evangelical." In view of this book's discussion, do you find the language useful and constructive—or not so much—to talk about a people interested in sharing and embodying the message of Jesus?
- Consider some examples of witness from religious groups and faiths different than your own. What do you learn from these? What do you admire about them?
- Consider the witness of your own life. Make a list of some of the most important ways you bear witness to your faith in everyday life, however subtly or in small ways.
- Consider the witness of your Christian community. Make a list of some of the most important ways your community bears witness to the faith of Jesus.

Bibliography

Abadi, Mark. "11 Dramatic Ways the World Has Changed in the Last 20 Years Alone." Business Insider, March 29, 2018. https://www.businessinsider.com/progress-innovation-since-1998-2018-3.

Adams, Edward. *The Earliest Christian Meeting Places: Almost Exclusively Houses?* Rev. ed. The Library of New Testament Studies 450. London: T. & T. Clark, 2016.

Alexander, Loveday. "Reading Luke-Acts from Back to Front." In *The Unity of Luke-Acts*, edited by J. Verheyden, 419–46. Bibliotheca Ephemeridum Theologicarum Lovaniensium 142. Leuven: Leuven University Press, 1999.

Aune, David E. *The New Testament in Its Literary Environment.* Library of Early Christianity. Philadelphia: Westminster, 1987.

Aymer, Margaret. "Exotica and the Ethiopian of Acts 8:26–40: Toward a Different Fabula." *Journal of Biblical Literature* 142.3 (2023) 533–46.

Barber, William J., II. "Foreword." In *Reconstructing the Gospel: Finding Freedom from Slaveholder Religion* by Jonathan Wilson-Hartgrove, 5–7. Downers Grove, IL: InterVarsity, 2018.

Barna. "51% of Churchgoers Don't Know of the Great Commission." March 27, 2018. https://www.barna.com/research/half-churchgoers-not-heard-great-commission/.

———. "Actions, Invitations, Storytelling—How Gen Z Approaches Evangelism." July 27, 2021. https://www.barna.com/research/gen-z-evangelism/.

———. "Atheism Doubles Among Generation Z." January 24, 2018. https://www.barna.com/research/atheism-doubles-among-generation-z/.

———. "Beyond an Invitation to Church: Opportunities for Faith-Sharing." March 26, 2019. https://www.barna.com/research/opportunities-for-faith-sharing/.

———. "Five Trends Defining Americans' Relationship to Churches." February 19, 2020. https://www.barna.com/research/current-perceptions/.

———. "Peace, Hope, Healing—What Spirituality Means to Americans Today." April 5, 2023. https://www.barna.com/research/spirituality-means/.

———. "Sharing Faith Is Increasingly Optional to Christians." May 15, 2018. https://www.barna.com/research/sharing-faith-increasingly-optional-christians/.

———. "What Makes an Engaging Witness, as Defined by Gen Z." November 10, 2021. https://www.barna.com/research/gen-z-witness/.

Bibliography

———. "Why People Are Reluctant to Discuss Faith." August 14, 2018. https://www.barna.com/research/reasons-for-reluctance/.

Barreto, Eric D. "Commentary on Acts 8:26–39." Working Preacher, May 7, 2017. https://www.workingpreacher.org/commentaries/narrative-lectionary/ethiopian-eunuch-baptized/commentary-on-acts-826-39.

———. "Negotiating Difference: Theology and Ethnicity in the Acts of the Apostles." *Word and World* 31.2 (Spring 2011) 129–37.

———. "What Happened at Pentecost?" Enter the Bible. https://enterthebible.org/what-happened-at-pentecost-eric-d-barreto.

Barrett, C. K. *A Critical and Exegetical Commentary on the Acts of the Apostles.* 2 vols. International Critical Commentary. London: T. & T. Clark, 1994.

———. "Paul's Speech on the Areopagus." In *New Testament Christianity for Africa and the World: Essays in Honour of Harry Sawyer*, edited by Mark E. Glasswell and Edward W. Fasholé-Luke, 69–77. London: SPCK, 1974.

Barrett, David P. Biblemapper Atlas, 2023. www.biblemapper.com.

Bass, Diana Butler, and J. Stewart-Sicking, eds. *From Nomads to Pilgrims: Stories from Practicing Congregations.* Washington, DC: Rowman & Littlefield, 2005.

Bateza, Anthony. "Beyond Evangelism: Sharing What Matters." *Living Lutheran*, March 26, 2024. https://www.livinglutheran.org/2024/03/beyond-evangelism-sharing-what-matters/.

Bauckham, Richard. "James and the Jerusalem Church." In *The Book of Acts in Its First Century Setting, Volume 4: The Book of Acts in Its Palestinian Setting*, edited by Richard Bauckham, 415–80. Grand Rapids: Eerdmans, 1995.

Bauer, David R. *The Book of Acts as Story: A Narrative-Critical Study.* Grand Rapids: Baker, 2021.

Ben Shahar, Meir. "Jewish Views of Gentiles." In *The Jewish Annotated New Testament*, edited by Amy-Jill Levine and Marc Zvi Brettler, 640–45. Rev. and enlarged ed. New York: Oxford University Press, 2018.

Bertram, Georg, and Karl Ludwig Schmidt. "ἔθνος, ἐθνικός." In *TDNT* 2:364–72.

Blezard, Robert C. "The 'E' Word: Why Does the ELCA Have the Word 'Evangelical' in Its Name?" *Living Lutheran*, April 6, 2018. https://www.livinglutheran.org/2018/04/the-e-word/.

Book of Concord: The Confessions of the Evangelical Lutheran Church. Edited by Robert Kolb and Timothy J. Wengert, translated by Charles Arand et al. Minneapolis: Fortress, 2000.

Borg, Marcus. "Faith: A Journey of Trust." Lenten Noonday Preaching Series. Calvary Episcopal Church, Memphis, Tennessee, 1999. http://www.explorefaith.org/faces/my_faith/borg/faith_by_marcus_borg.php.

Bowen, John. *Evangelism for "Normal" People: Good News for Those Looking for a Fresh Approach.* Minneapolis: Augsburg Fortress, 2002.

Branick, Victor. *The House Church in the Writings of Paul.* Eugene, OR: Wipf & Stock, 2012.

Burke, Sean D. "Queering Early Christian Discourse: The Ethiopian Eunuch." In *Bible Trouble: Queer Readings at the Boundary of Biblical Scholarship*, edited by Teresa J. Hornsby and Ken Stone, 175–89. Semeia Studies 67. Atlanta: Society of Biblical Literature, 2011.

Chadwick, Henry. *The Early Church.* London: Penguin, 1968.

Childs, David. *The Fall of the GDR: Germany's Road to Unity.* New York: Routledge, 2014.

Bibliography

Claiborne, Shane, and Jonathan Wilson-Hartgrove. *Becoming the Answer to Our Prayers: Prayer for Ordinary Radicals*. Downers Grove, IL: InterVarsity, 2018.

Cohn, D'Vera, and Andrea Caumont. "10 Demographic Trends Shaping the U.S. and the World in 2016." Pew Research Center, March 31, 2016. https://www.pewresearch.org/short-reads/2016/03/31/10-demographic-trends-that-are-shaping-the-u-s-and-the-world/.

Conde-Frazier, Elizabeth. *Atando Cabos: Latinx Contributions to Theological Education*. Grand Rapids: Eerdmans, 2021.

Conzelmann, Hans. *Acts of the Apostles: A Commentary on the Acts of the Apostles*. Translated by James Limburg, A. Thomas Kraabel, and Donald H. Juel. Hermeneia. Philadelphia: Fortress, 1987.

———. "The Address of Paul on the Areopagus." In *Studies in Luke-Acts: Essays in Honor of Paul Schubert*, edited by John Knox, 217–30. Nashville: Abingdon, 1966.

Curry, Andrew. "We Are the People: A Peaceful Revolution in Leipzig." *Spiegel*, October 9, 2009. https://www.spiegel.de/international/germany/we-are-the-people-a-peaceful-revolution-in-leipzig-a-654137.html.

Daniel, Jerry L. "Anti-Semitism in the Hellenistic-Roman Period." *Journal of Biblical Literature* 98.1 (1979) 45–65.

Daniel, Lillian. *Tell It Like It Is: Reclaiming the Practice of Testimony*. Herndon, VA: Alban Institute, 2006.

Danker, Frederick W., Walter Bauer, William F. Arndt, and F. Wilbur Gingrich. *Greek-English Lexicon of the New Testament and Other Early Christian Literature*. 3rd ed. Chicago: University of Chicago Press, 2000.

Darling, Don. "'Evangelical' Is a Term With Heavy Baggage. But Christians Shouldn't Give Up On It." *USA Today*, July 9, 2021. https://www.usatoday.com/story/opinion/2021/07/09/why-christians-shouldnt-give-up-term-evangelical-politics/7885447002/.

Daubert, Dave. "A Cure for Lutheran Laryngitis? Here's What It Means to Be Lutheran Today." *The Lutheran*, August 2007. http://www.thelutheran.org/article/article.cfm?article_id=6612.

———. "Evangelism 101: What Do You Really Need to Know?" Presentation to the Southeastern Synod of the ELCA, January 30, 2022. https://www.youtube.com/watch?v=OFkSju4qi5E.

———. *The Invitational Christian*. Elgin, IL: Day 8 Strategies, 2017.

Day, Keri. "The Collective Act of Testifying." *In Trust* 33.1 (Autumn 2021) 16–19.

———. *Notes of a Native Daughter: Testifying in Theological Education*. Grand Rapids: Eerdmans, 2021.

Deferrari, Roy J., trans. *The New Fathers of the Church: A New Translation*. Washington, DC: Catholic University of America, 1953.

Dibelius, Martin. "Paul on the Areopagus." In *Studies in the Acts of the Apostles*, edited by Heinrich Greeven, translated by Mary Ling, 26–77. London: SCM, 1956.

Diggle, J., et al., eds. *The Cambridge Greek Lexicon*. 2 vols. Cambridge: Cambridge University Press, 2021.

Dube, Zorodzai. "The Ethiopian Eunuch in Transit: A Migrant Theoretical Perspective." *Harvard Theological Studies* 69.1 (Jan. 2013) 1–7. http://dx.doi.org/10.4102/hts.v69i1.2019.

Dunn, James D. G. *The Acts of the Apostles*. Grand Rapids: Eerdmans, 1996.

BIBLIOGRAPHY

Dupertuis, Rubén R. "The Summaries of Acts 2, 4, and 5 and Plato's Republic." In *Ancient Fiction: The Matrix of Early Christian and Jewish Narrative*, edited by JoAnn A. Brant, Charles W. Hedrick, and Chris Shea, 275–95. Atlanta: Society of Biblical Literature, 2005.

Dupont, Jacques. "The Salvation of the Gentiles." In *The Salvation of the Gentiles: Essays on the Acts of the Apostles*, 11–34. Mahwah, NJ: Paulist, 1979.

Engelhart, L. B. *How the World Has Changed: What We Should Have Learned: A Journey Through Fifty Years of Technology, Social Development, and Human Experience*. Independently published, 2023.

Epictetus. *Discourses*. Translated by William Abbott Oldfather. Loeb Classical Library 131. Cambridge: Harvard University Press, 1956.

Falk, Daniel K. "Jewish Prayer Literature and the Jerusalem Church in Acts." In *The Book of Acts in Its First Century Setting, Volume 4: The Book of Acts in Its Palestinian Setting*, edited by Richard Bauckham, 267–301. Grand Rapids: Eerdmans, 1995.

Feldman, Louis H. "Conversion to Judaism in Classical Antiquity." *Hebrew Union College Annual* 74 (2003) 115–56.

Fields, Uriah J. *Montgomery Bus Boycott: In a Nutshell—a Chronology*. Independently published, 2018.

Fitzmyer, Joseph A. *The Acts of the Apostles*. Anchor Bible 31. New York: Doubleday, 1998.

Flood, David, and Thadée Matura, eds. *The Birth of a Movement: A Study of the First Rule of St Francis*. Chicago: Franciscan Herald Press, 1975. https://www.capdox.capuchin.org.au/legislation/the-unconfirmed-first-rule-of-st-francis/.

Freedman, David Noel, ed. *Anchor Bible Dictionary*. 6 vols. New York: Doubleday, 1992.

Fryer, Kelly A. *Reclaiming the "E" Word: Waking Up to Our Evangelical Identity*. Lutheran Voices. Minneapolis: Augsburg, 2008.

———, ed. *A Story Worth Sharing: Engaging Evangelism*. Minneapolis: Augsburg Fortress, 2004.

Funkhouser, Sara A. "Freed to Proclaim: Evangelism and Discipleship." *Currents in Theology and Mission* 49.2 (Apr. 2022) 38–41.

Gaiser, Frederick J. "What Luther *Didn't* Say About Vocation." *Word and World* 25.4 (Fall 2005) 359–61.

Gamble, Harry Y. *Books and Readers in the Early Church: A History of Early Christian Texts*. New Haven, CT: Yale University Press, 1995.

Gärtner, B. *The Areopagus Speech and Natural Revelation*. Acta Seminarii Neotestamentici Upsaliensis 21. Uppsala: Almqvist & Wiksell, 1955.

Gaventa, Beverly Roberts. *Acts*. Abingdon New Testament Commentaries. Nashville: Abingdon, 2003.

———. *From Darkness to Light: Aspects of Conversion in the New Testament*. Overtures to Biblical Theology. Philadelphia: Fortress, 1986.

———. "Traditions in Conversation and Collision: Reflections on Multiculturalism in the Acts of the Apostles." In *Making Room at the Table: An Invitation to Multicultural Worship*, edited by Brian K. Blount and Leonora Tubbs Tisdale, 30–41. Louisville: Westminster John Knox, 2001.

Giere, S. D. *Freedom and Imagination: Trusting Christ in an Age of Bad Faith*. Minneapolis: Fortress, 2023.

Glassman, Bernie. *Bearing Witness: A Zen Master's Lessons in Making Peace*. New York: Harmony, 1998.

Bibliography

Global Friends Coalition. "The Response to the Events at Juba Coffee and Restaurant." In *Global Friends Coalition Annual Report*, 7. 2015. http://www.gfcoalition.org/uploads/1/0/3/0/10308081/gfc_annual_report_2015_final.pdf.

González, Justo L. *The Story Luke Tells: Luke's Unique Witness to the Gospel*. Grand Rapids: Eerdmans, 2015.

———. *The Story of Christianity*. 2 vols. San Francisco: Harper, 1984.

Goodman, Martin. "Jewish Proselytizing in the First Century." In *The Jews Among Pagans and Christians in the Roman Empire*, edited by Judith Lieu, John North, and Tessa Rajak, 53–78. New York: Routledge, 1992.

Gutenson, Charles E. *The Right Church: Live Like the First Christians*. Nashville: Abingdon, 2012.

Haenchen, Ernst. *The Acts of the Apostles: A Commentary*. Translated by Bernard Noble et al. Oxford: Basil Blackwell, 1971.

Hanson, Mark S. *Faithful Yet Changing: The Church in Challenging Times*. Minneapolis: Augsburg Fortress, 2002.

Hornblower, Simon, and Antony Spawforth, eds. *Oxford Classical Dictionary*. 4th ed. Oxford: Oxford University Press, 2012.

Hoyt, Thomas, Jr. "Testimony." In *Practicing Our Faith: A Way of Life for a Searching People*, edited by Dorothy C. Bass, 91–103. San Francisco: Jossey-Bass, 1997.

Hull, J. H. E. *The Holy Spirit in the Acts of the Apostles*. London: Lutterworth, 1967.

Jacobson, Harold. *Rockin' the Front Porch: Sharing the Faith in the New Normal*. Morrisville, NC: Lulu, 2020.

Jennings, Willie James. *Acts*. Belief: A Theological Commentary on the Bible. Louisville: Westminster John Knox, 2017.

Jervell, Jacob. "The Church of Jews and Godfearers." In *Luke-Acts and the Jewish People: Eight Critical Perspectives*, edited by Joseph B. Tyson, 11–20. Minneapolis: Augsburg, 1988.

Johnson, Judith. "The Power of Bearing Witness." *Huffington Post*, September 21, 2010 (rev. November 17, 2011). https://www.huffpost.com/entry/the-power-of-bearing-witn_b_721210.

Johnson, Luke Timothy. *Prophetic Jesus, Prophetic Church: The Challenge of Luke-Acts to Contemporary Christians*. Grand Rapids: Eerdmans, 2011.

Just, Felix. "New Testament Statistics." 2005. https://catholic-resources.org/Bible/NT-Statistics-Greek.htm.

Kaiser, Walter C., Jr. *Mission in the Old Testament: Israel as a Light to the Nations*. Grand Rapids: Baker, 2000.

Kerns, Thomas A., and Kathleen Dean Moore, eds. *Bearing Witness: The Human Rights Case Against Fracking and Climate Change*. Corvallis: Oregon State University Press, 2021.

Keener, Craig S. "Acts 10: Were Troops Stationed in Caesarea During Agrippa's Rule?" *Journal of Greco-Roman Christianity and Judaism* 7 (2010) 164–76.

———. *Acts: An Exegetical Commentary*. 4 vols. Grand Rapids: Baker, 2012–15.

Khan, Dan'el. "The Queen Mother in the Kingdom of Kush: Status, Power and Cultic Role." In *Teshura le-Zafrira: Studies in the Bible, the History of Israel, and the Ancient Near East Presented to Zafrira Ben-Barak of the University of Haifa*, edited by Mayer I. Gruber et al., 61–68. Beersheva: Ben Gurion University of the Negev, 2012.

Bibliography

King, Martin Luther, Jr. "The Montgomery Bus Boycott" (1955). BlackPast, January 17, 2012. https://www.blackpast.org/african-american-history/1955-martin-luther-king-jr-montgomery-bus-boycott/.

Kittel, Gerhard, and Gerhard Friedrich, eds. *Theological Dictionary of the New Testament*. Translated by Geoffrey W. Bromiley. 10 vols. Grand Rapids: Eerdmans, 1964–76.

Kozek, Cindie. *Globe Is Changing for a Much Better Place: Data About the World in Terms of Health, Wealth, and More*. Amazon: May 9, 2021.

Lindemann, Andreas. "The Beginnings of Christian Life in Jerusalem According to the Summaries in the Acts of the Apostles (Acts 2:42–47; 4:32–37; 5:12–16)." In *Common Life in the Early Church: Essays Honoring Graydon F. Snyder*, edited by Julian V. Hills, 202–18. Harrisburg, PA: Trinity, 1998.

Littman, Robert. "Antisemitism in the Greco-Roman Pagan World." In *Remembering for the Future, Volume 1: Jews and Christians During and After the Holocaust*, 825–35. Oxford: Pergamon, 1989.

Long, Thomas G. *Testimony: Talking Ourselves into Being Christian*. Hoboken, NJ: Jossey-Bass, 2003.

Luther, Martin. *Luther's Works*. American ed. Edited by Jaroslav Pelikan and Helmut Lehmann. 55 vols. St. Louis and Philadelphia: Concordia and Fortress, 1955–86.

———. *D. Martin Luthers Werke: Kritische Gesamtausgabe*. 127 vols. Weimar: Hermann Böhlaus Nachfolger, 1883–1980.

Malherbe, Abraham J., ed. *The Cynic Epistles: A Study Edition*. Missoula, MT: Scholars, 1977.

———. *Paul and the Thessalonians: The Philosophic Tradition of Pastoral Care*. Philadelphia: Fortress, 1987.

Manguel, Alberto. *A History of Reading*. New York: Penguin, 1997.

Marguerat, Daniel. *Les Actes des Apôtres Commentaire du Nouveau Testament (1–12)*. Geneva: Labor et Fides, 2015.

Marshall, I. Howard, and David Peterson, eds. *Witness to the Gospel: The Theology of Acts*. Grand Rapids: Eerdmans, 1998.

Mattill, A. J., Jr. "The Jesus-Paul Parallels and the Purpose of Luke-Acts: H. H. Evans Reconsidered." *Novum Testamentum* 17.1 (1975) 15–46.

Meador, Jake. "The Misunderstood Reason Millions of Americans Stopped Going to Church." *Atlantic*, July 2023. https://www.theatlantic.com/ideas/archive/2023/07/christian-church-communitiy-participation-drop/674843/.

Mealand, D. L. "The Close of Acts and Its Hellenistic Greek Vocabulary." *New Testament Studies* 36 (Oct. 1990) 592–96.

Metzger, Bruce. *A Textual Commentary on the Greek New Testament*. 2nd ed. Freiburg im Breisgau: United Bible Societies, 1994.

Miles, Sara. *City of God: Faith in the Streets*. Alexandria, VA: Jericho, 2015.

Moloney, Francis J. *Witnesses to the Ends of the Earth: New Testament Reflections on Mission*. Mahwah, NJ: Paulist, 2022.

MPR News. "Minnesota Man Convicted of Hate Crime for Cafe Fire Receives 15 Years." September 7, 2016. https://www.mprnews.org/story/2016/09/07/hate-crime-matthew-gust.

Nessan, Craig L. "After the Death of Evangelism—The Resurrection of an Evangelizing Church." In *The Evangelizing Church: A Lutheran Contribution*, edited by Richard H. Bliese and Craig Van Gelder, 113–32. Minneapolis: Augsburg Fortress, 2005.

Bibliography

———. "My Take: Tear Down Magical Walls." *Living Lutheran*, July 9, 2021. https://www.livinglutheran.org/2021/07/my-take-tear-down-magical-walls/.
Nouwen, Henri J. M. *Discernment: Reading the Signs of Daily Life*. Edited by Michael J. Christensen and Rebecca J. Laird. San Francisco: HarperOne, 2013.
———. *Here and Now: Living in the Spirit*. New York: Crossroad, 1995.
———. *Spiritual Direction: Wisdom for the Long Walk of Faith*. Edited by Michael J. Christensen and Rebecca J. Laird. San Francisco: HarperOne, 2006.
———. *The Wounded Healer: Ministry in Contemporary Society*. New York: Image, 2013.
Orlinsky, Harry M. "'A Light of the Nations': A Problem in Biblical Theology." In *The Seventy-Fifth Anniversary Volume of the Jewish Quarterly Review*, 131–43. Philadelphia: Jewish Quarterly Review, 1967.
O'Toole, Robert F. "Activity of the Risen Jesus in Luke-Acts." *Biblica* 62 (1981) 471–98.
———. *The Christological Climax of Paul's Defense (Ac. 22:1—26:32)*. Analecta Biblica 78. Rome: Biblical Institute, 1978.
———. "Parallels Between Jesus and His Disciples in Luke-Acts: A Further Study." *Biblische Zeitschrift* 27.2 (1983) 195–212.
Parsons, Mikeal C. *Body and Character: The Subversion of Physiognomy in Early Christianity*. Waco, TX: Baylor University Press, 2011.
———. *The Departure of Jesus in Luke-Acts: The Ascension Narratives in Context*. Journal for the Study of the New Testament Supplement Series. Sheffield: Sheffield Academic Press, 1988.
Parsons, Mikeal C., and Richard I. Pervo. *Rethinking the Unity of Luke and Acts*. Minneapolis: Fortress, 1993.
Peterson, Cheryl M. *Who Is the Church? An Ecclesiology for the Twenty-First Century*. Minneapolis: Fortress, 2013.
Peterson, Eugene H. *The Contemplative Pastor: Returning to the Art of Spiritual Direction*. The Leadership Library 17. Carol Stream, IL: Christianity Today, 1989.
———. "What Faith Looks Like Outside the Church." Laity Lodge video interview, July 15, 2008. https://www.youtube.com/watch?v=RENec9hbG4o.
Pew Research Center. "Religious 'Nones' in America: Who They Are and What They Believe." January 24, 2024. https://pewrsr.ch/3SedVTm.
Pikiewicz, Kristi. "The Power and Strength of Bearing Witness." *Psychology Today*, December 1, 2013. https://www.psychologytoday.com/us/blog/meaningful-you/201312/the-power-and-strength-bearing-witness.
Plato. *The Apology of Socrates*. Translated by Benjamin Jowett, adapted by Miriam Carlisle et al. Center for Hellenic Studies, November 2, 2020. https://chs.harvard.edu/primary-source/plato-the-apology-of-socrates-sb/.
Public Religion Research Institute Staff. "PRRI 2021 Census of American Religion, Updates and Trends." April 27, 2022. https://www.prri.org/spotlight/prri-2021-american-values-atlas-religious-affiliation-updates-and-trends-white-christian-decline-slows-unaffiliated-growth-levels-off/.
Pythian-Adams, W. J. "The Problem of 'Deserted' Gaza." *Palestine Exploration Fund Quarterly Statement* (1923) 30–36.
Reed, Angela H. "Spiritual Discernment in the Congregation." *Vision* (Winnipeg) 17.1 (2016) 46–53.
Richardson, Allissa V. *Bearing Witness While Black: African Americans, Smartphones, and the New Protest #Journalism*. Oxford: Oxford University Press, 2021.

Bibliography

Rinehart, Michael. "The Peaceful Revolution, October 9, 1989." *Bishop Michael Rinehart* (blog), October 8, 2022. https://bishopmike.com/2022/10/08/the-peaceful-revolution-october-9-1989/.

Roberts, Alexander, and James Donaldson, eds. *The Ante-Nicene Fathers*. 10 vols. 1885–1887. Repr., Grand Rapids: Eerdmans, 1951.

Rothschild, Clare K. *Paul in Athens: The Popular Religious Context of Acts 17*. Wissenschaftliche Untersuchungen zum Neuen Testament 341. Tübingen: Mohr Siebeck, 2014.

Saldarini, Anthony J. "Sanhedrin." In *ABD* 5:975–80.

Sampley, J. Paul. "Paul's Frank Speech with the Galatians and the Corinthians." In *Philodemus and the New Testament World*, edited by John T. Fitzgerald, Dirk Obbink, and Glenn Holland, 295–321. Supplements to Novum Testamentum 111. Leiden: Brill, 2003.

Schertz, Mary H. "'This Was Not Done in a Corner': Lessons on Proclamation from the Book of Acts." *Vision* (Winnipeg) 18.2 (Fall 2017) 86–93.

Schneider, Johannes. "εὐνοῦχος, εὐνουχίζω." In *TDNT* 2:765–68.

Schöne, Jens. *The Peaceful Revolution: Berlin 1989/90—The Path to German Unity*. Berlin: Berlin Story, 2009.

Schubert, Paul S. "The Place of the Areopagus Speech in the Composition of Acts." In *Transitions in Biblical Scholarship*, edited by J. Coert Rylaarsdam, 235–61. Chicago: University of Chicago Press, 1968.

Scott, Emily M. D. *For All Who Hunger: Searching for Communion in a Shattered World*. Colorado Springs: Convergent, 2020.

Skinner, Matthew L. *Acts: Catching Up With the Spirit*. Nashville: Abingdon, 2020.

Smallwood, E. Mary. *The Jews Under Roman Rule: From Pompey to Diocletian—a Study in Political Relations*. Leiden: Brill Academic, 2001.

Smith, Gregory A. "About Three-in-Ten U.S. Adults Are Now Religiously Unaffiliated." Pew Research Center, December 14, 2021. https://www.pewresearch.org/religion/2021/12/14/about-three-in-ten-u-s-adults-are-now-religiously-unaffiliated/.

Smith, Gregory A., and Alan Cooperman. "Has the Rise of Religious 'Nones' Come to an End in the U.S.?" Pew Research Center, January 24, 2024. https://www.pewresearch.org/short-reads/2024/01/24/has-the-rise-of-religious-nones-come-to-an-end-in-the-us/.

Smith, Peter. "America's Nonreligious Are a Growing, Diverse Phenomenon. They Really Don't Like Organized Religion." Associated Press News, October 4, 2023. https://apnews.com/article/nonreligious-united-states-nones-spirituality-humanist-91bb8430280c88fd88530a7ad64b03f8.

Smith, Robert Houston. "Ethiopia." In *ABD* 2:665–68.

Soards, Marion L. *The Speeches in Acts: Their Content, Contexts, and Concerns*. Louisville: Westminster John Knox, 1994.

Spencer, F. Scott. "The Ethiopian Eunuch and His Bible: A Social-Science Analysis." *Biblical Theology Bulletin* 22.4 (Winter 1992) 155–65.

———. *The Portrait of Philip in Acts: A Study of Roles and Relations*. The Library of New Testament Studies. London: T. & T. Clark, 1992.

Strathmann, H. "μάρτυς, μαρτυρέω, μαρτυρία, μαρτύριον." In *TDNT* 4:474–514.

Tacitus. *The Histories of Tacitus IV–V*. Translated by Clifford H. Moore. Loeb Classical Library 249. Cambridge: Harvard University Press, 1931.

Bibliography

Talbert, Charles H. *Literary Patterns, Theological Themes, and the Genre of Luke-Acts.* Society of Biblical Literature Monograph Series 20. Missoula, MT: Scholars, 1974.

Tannehill, Robert C. *The Narrative Unity of Luke-Acts: A Literary Interpretation.* 2 vols. Minneapolis: Fortress, 1990–94.

Thomason, Steve. *A Cartoonist's Guide to Acts: A Full-Color Graphic Novel.* A Cartoonist's Guide to the Bible. Self-published, 2023.

Tiede, David L. "The Conversion of the Church." *Currents in Theology and Mission* 33.1 (2006) 42–51.

Toner, Jerry. *Popular Culture in Ancient Rome.* Malden, MA: Polity, 2009.

Trites, Allison A. *The New Testament Concept of Witness.* Society for New Testament Studies Monograph Series 31. Cambridge: Cambridge University Press, 1977.

Troftgruben, Troy M. *A Conclusion Unhindered: A Study of the Ending of Acts Within Its Literary Environment.* Wissenschaftliche Untersuchungen zum Neuen Testament 2.280. Tübingen: Mohr Siebeck, 2010.

———. "The Ending of Luke Revisited." *Journal of Biblical Literature* 140.2 (2021) 325–46.

Turner, Max. "Every Believer as a Witness in Acts?—In Dialogue with John Michael Penney." *Ashland Theological Journal* 30 (1998) 57–71.

Tyson, Joseph B. "The Problem of Jewish Rejection in Luke-Acts." In *Luke-Acts and the Jewish People: Eight Critical Perspectives*, edited by Joseph B. Tyson, 124–37. Minneapolis: Augsburg, 1988.

Van Unnik, W. C. "The 'Book of Acts': The Confirmation of the Gospel." *Novum Testamentum* 4.1 (1960) 26–59.

———. "The Christian's Freedom of Speech in the New Testament." *Bulletin of the John Rylands University Library of Manchester* 44.2 (1962) 466–88.

Walter, Patricia. *The Assumed Authorial Unity of Luke and Acts: A Reassessment of the Evidence.* Society of New Testament Studies Monograph Series 145. Cambridge: Cambridge University Press, 2009.

Walton, Steve. "Deciding About Deciding: Early Christian Communal Decision-Making in Acts." In *Reading Acts Theologically*, 89–106. The Library of New Testament Series 661. London: T. & T. Clark, 2022.

———. "Primitive Communism in Acts? Does Acts Present the Community of Goods (2:44–45; 4:32–35) as Mistaken?" In *Reading Acts Theologically*, 63–73. The Library of New Testament Series 661. London: T. & T. Clark, 2022.

———. "What Does 'Mission' in Acts Mean in Relation to the 'Powers That Be'?" In *Reading Acts Theologically*, 123–42. The Library of New Testament Series 661. London: T. & T. Clark, 2022.

Williams, C. S. C. *A Commentary on the Acts of the Apostles.* Harper's New Testament Commentaries. New York: Harper & Row, 1957.

Williams, Rowan. *Being Christian: Baptism, Bible, Eucharist, Prayer.* Grand Rapids: Eerdmans, 2014.

Wilson, Brittany E. "'Neither Male Nor Female': The Ethiopian Eunuch in Acts 8.26–40." *New Testament Studies* 60 (2014) 403–22.

———. *Unmanly Men: Refigurations of Masculinity in Luke-Acts.* Oxford: Oxford University Press, 2015.

Wilson, Stephen. *The Gentiles and the Gentile Mission in Luke-Acts.* Society for New Testament Studies Monograph Series 23. Cambridge: Cambridge University Press, 1973.

Woofenden, Anna. *This Is God's Table: Finding Church Beyond the Walls.* Harrisonburg, VA: Herald, 2020.

Bibliography

Yamauchi, Edwin M. "Acts 8:26–40: Why the Ethiopian Eunuch Was Not from Ethiopia." In *Interpreting the New Testament Text: Introduction to the Art and Science of Exegesis*, edited by Darrell L. Bock and Buist M. Fanning, 351–66. Wheaton, IL: Crossway, 2006.

Yoo, Joseph. "How Is It With Your Soul?" *Ministry Matters*, August 2, 2016. https://www.ministrymatters.com/lead/entry/7571/how-is-it-with-your-soul.

Zerzan, Rebecca. "How Has the World Changed in the Last 20 Years?" United Nations Population Fund, April 7, 2014. https://www.unfpa.org/news/how-has-world-changed-last-20-years.

www.ingramcontent.com/pod-product-compliance
Lightning Source LLC
Chambersburg PA
CBHW030112170426
43198CB00009B/600